# CAREER C
## JOB SEAR(

# CAREER CHOICE JOB SEARCH

GUIDENOTES
for
GRADUATES
and
PROFESSIONALS

## SANDER MEREDEEN

HARCOURT BRACE JOVANOVICH,
PUBLISHERS
London   Orlando   Sydney   Toronto

Harcourt Brace Jovanovich Limited
24/28 Oval Road, London NW1 7DX

ISBN: 0-7466-9900-X (cased)
      0-7466-9905-0 (paperback)

Typeset by Photo·graphics Ltd and
printed by Mackays of Chatham PLC, Chatham, Kent

British Library Cataloguing in Publication Data are available.
First published 1990

*Acknowledgements*

The publishers wish to thank Abbey National plc, ICI plc, Virgin Group Ltd, The Levitt Group Ltd, the City of Birmingham Symphony Orchestra (photographer: Alan Wood), Jonathan Cape (Miriam Berkeley), Brook Street Bureau, Meyer International plc, Sock Shop International plc, and Munro and Forster Public Relations Ltd (photographer: Trevor Leighton) for supplying photographs of 'high-flyers'.

*For my sixteen first cousins*
*—whose careers flourish mightily—*

*Barrie*
*David, Helena and Aron*
*Judy and Naomi*
*Colin, Brian and Martin*
*Jennifer, Hilary and Arnold*
*Carmel and Rina*
*Michael and Madeleine*

*and for my second cousins*
*—too numerous to name—*
*whose careers have scarcely begun*

*—with deep affection—*

*Setting out on the voyage to Ithaca you must pray that the way be long, full of adventures and experiences.*

C. P. Cafavy: *Ithaca* (1911)

# Contents

# ━━━━━ **Foreword** ━━━━━

Commander Desmond Warren-Evans DSO, RNVR (Retired) fixed me with one nautically-trained eye, scanning my papers with the other: 'So, you want to go into personnel work?' barked the LSE's full-time Careers Adviser. 'That seems to be this year's fashion. Last year it was journalism, this year it's personnel. My advice to you, Meredeen, is to take a postgraduate Diploma in Accounting. That's the up-and-coming profession.'

It was 1956—the year of Suez and Hungary—and just one month from finals. I thanked the Commander, walked out of his office, out of the LSE and into the world of work. I've no means of knowing, of course, what my life's work might have been had I followed the Commander's advice. But I'm glad I did *not* train as an accountant!

How fortunate are those who are *certain* about their future life's work! If you've successfully completed (or are about to complete) your course and have done some sensible career planning, you're doubly fortunate! All you need now is an attractive employment offer in your chosen specialist field—and your career is launched.

The best-paid jobs and the most rewarding careers, throughout the 1990s and into the 21st century, will undoubtedly go to graduates and professionals who are wise enough to make an early career choice and then stick to it. The majority will go on to build successful— perhaps brilliant—careers in the years ahead. Most of us are less fortunate. We proceed by trial and error, sometimes making costly mistakes, stumbling into our careers by chance. We may take years to discover what we're best at, what we *really* want to do with our lives. And some of us make that discovery too late.

No life experience need ever be wasted. But if you hope to be a successful ballet dancer, athlete or musician—if you're destined for medicine, dentistry, accountancy, engineering or the law—you'd better start young and steel yourself for several years of professional training. *You can always change your job—but not your career. Your career choice and job search should therefore start before you leave college or university.*

This book owes its inspiration to my students at the LSE and at Strathclyde University who continue to consult me about their careers. When I ask them why, they say that I teach Human Resource Management from the basis of academic theory plus a detailed practical knowledge of the world beyond the university—a dark and dangerous world only dimly perceived by my more scholarly academic colleagues. How right my students are!

Leaving school at 18, I earned my first pay packet (£2 per day) as a Supply Teacher in East London. During the next two years' National Service in the Royal Navy, I never earned as much again. Then, after four vegetable years as an Executive Officer in the Ministry of Education, I quit the Civil Service at 25 to read for a degree at the LSE. The Commissioners wrote to point out that by resigning I would forfeit my three years' non-contributory accrued pension rights and would be giving up a secure salary of £450 per annum. I thanked them politely and left.

In 1956, aged 28, I graduated with first class honours in Economics and Political Science and was offered an Assistant Lecturership at the LSE at £750 per annum. Instead, I chose to join British Steel at £850 per annum with a burning ambition to earn £1000 by the age of 30—perhaps £20 000 by today's standards. And I only just made it!

After 20 years' experience of personnel management and industrial relations in British Steel and the Ford Motor Company, I returned to the LSE at 48 to read for a Masters Degree in Human Resource Management, staying on to teach that subject for the next 13 years, first at the LSE and latterly at Strathclyde Business School. During this period I have taught, advised, researched, counselled, written, published, broadcast and consulted widely in the private and public sectors, finding still wider sources of personal growth, development and fulfilment.

Having retired from full-time teaching at 60, with an Honorary Fellowship at the University of Strathclyde's Centre for Academic Practice, I intended to devote most of my energies to research and writing. Instead, I find myself spending more and more time on *Career Choice and Job Search*—an independent careers counselling service which I established with a colleague four years ago at Strathclyde Business School, to help university graduates and others with professional qualifications to think more critically and positively about themselves *before* launching their careers. That counselling service now extends beyond Strathclyde University and includes professionals of many different kinds. In addition to my work as a career counsellor and management consultant, I have travelled and taught widely in the United States, written and published three further books, and have recently opened a new chapter in my career by presenting a variety of programmes for Radio Clyde, Scotland's most successful independent radio station.

This book will justify its existence if it helps graduates and others to sharpen their thinking before making their career decisions, thereby launching themselves into better jobs and more rewarding careers.

My sincere thanks are due to Christine Macpherson, Ian Easton, Roberta Fraser and Barbara Cohen for reading the manuscript and for offering their constructive comments. Without their generous help, this book would be much less readable. Responsibility for persistent errors and infelicities is mine.

*Bowen Craig*
*Largs*

# chapter 1

# Introduction:
# So, you're seeking paid
# employment?

*Work with all the ease and speed you can without breaking
your head.*

John Dryden (1631–1700)

These practical *Guidenotes* are addressed to all job
hunters everywhere—more specifically to those of you
who are about to leave university, polytechnic or college
(including some still in your final school year)—all those
who stand on the tiptoe of expectation—the very
springboard of your careers—and who, understandably
enough, feel anxious about taking the first plunge into
the dangerous unknown. These *Guidenotes* assume
that you've successfully completed (or will shortly
complete) a course of studies that has helped you,
broadly or narrowly, to prepare for some form of paid
employment. They also assume, rightly or wrongly, that
you really *are* looking for paid employment!

# WHO WANTS WORK, ANYWAY?

Parents and teachers, family and friends, economists and politicians—
yes, even the Secretary of State for Employment, whose Department
collates the monthly employment figures—all assume that every young
person about to leave college, and still of reasonably sound mind, will
be enthusiastically seeking paid employment. From their own peculiar
standpoints, that might seem a perfectly safe assumption. Most, though
not necessarily all, graduates will probably conform with that
expectation. But consider Brian's story.

## Brian's story

Brian had a wonderful time at college. Elder of two sons of a
comfortable family, he went to the University of Kent at Canterbury
straight from school to read for a degree in Law. He was uncertain
quite what that entailed and was even less sure that he really wanted
to be a lawyer or indeed whether he was suited for the legal
profession. In practice, he found himself bored by the technicalities
of 'lawyer's law' and became much more interested in law as an
instrument of social control.

Brian joined his college Labour Club, stood for office and was
eventually elected Sabbatical Treasurer of the Student Union. Despite
taking a sabbatical year off for these and other extracurricular
activities, Brian graduated with a 2(i) BA Degree in Law. He left
college in high spirits with an enviable degree of self-confidence and
a much-enhanced range of social and political skills. Parental
expectations were that he might now complete a postgraduate legal
qualification before deciding which branch of the legal profession to
enter.

To everyone's surprise Brian announced that, having spent four
hectic years on campus, he did not intend to undertake any further
studies but he was equally unprepared to settle down into regular
paid employment. For the next six months he lived at home, paying
his way by washing vehicles at a local car-hire firm.

Only then was he ready to begin looking seriously for paid
employment. He joined the Personnel Department of an international
engineering company and, five years later, transferred to the BBC,
where he now holds a middle management position as Personnel
Administrator in Broadcasting House, London. His knowledge of
labour law and his communication skills are both invaluable assets
in his work, which he finds both challenging and rewarding.

Brian may not be typical of graduates. Yet many will share his initial uncertainty about their choice of a career. And many more will understand his reluctance to plunge immediately into paid employment after the relative freedom of four years of college life. Statistics nevertheless show that, sooner rather than later, *virtually all graduates are also job hunters*. They seek paid employment for a combination of three principal reasons:

- *First*, most obviously and immediately, they need to start earning some money.

- *Second*, less obviously but no less immediately, they want to put their freshly-honed intelligence, skills and knowledge to some useful purpose.

- *Third*, least obviously perhaps, they want to put their feet on the first rungs of their chosen career ladder.

If you're impatient to put your foot on that ladder, you may be tempted to skip the rest of this *Introduction* together with Chapter 2 on careers, labour markets and how they interact. *We advise you not to do so*. Yet, throughout this book, we'll also encourage you to trust your judgement and decide for yourself when you're ready to move on!

We shall return more than once to that familiar, overworked metaphor of the career as a ladder with a series of differentially-spaced rungs which must be scaled in order to attain some significant place in the social, economic and professional pecking order. A ladder is a powerful symbol and a useful instrument: a means to an end—never an end in itself. Nobody want to be left half-way up a ladder. Yet no matter which career we choose, no matter how high our career aspirations, we almost invariably start at the bottom rung of the organizational hierarchy. And there's only way way to move: UP! Unless, that is, Daddy happens to be Chairman. But then, any good Chairman—and any sensible Daddy—might reasonably expect his offspring or potential successors to start at the bottom, where he says he started, and work their way up—as he triumphantly has done.

## WORK AS A CENTRAL LIFE INTEREST

Our essential starting point—and let's acknowledge it freely—is that, for a series of complex philosophical, religious, ethical, historical and cultural reasons, *work is now a central life interest*—perhaps *the* central life interest—for the vast majority of young men and women who have survived any form of tertiary education—and who are not already the heirs to a substantial fortune!

Of course, it's possible to identify a handful of graduates in all the arts and sciences who drop out and go to live on the beach in Tahiti, Tenerife or Tighnabruaich—where, incidentally, the concept of work as a central life interest is catching on fast! Most young men and women who have recently completed a course of studies at college or university continue to exhibit an apparently insatiable appetite for art and literature, for poetry and politics, for music, drama and dancing, for sex and love, for food and drink, for clothes and cars—yes, even for computers! Yet their all-consuming, all-encompassing passion—the one idea which they carry with them from graduation to the grave—long after the sex-drive has diminished, the spouse has disappeared and the children have flown the nest—is their daily work, their paid employment—in short, their careers. *This book is for them—and for you.* It encapsulates the essence of the author's life experience—most of it spent in learning how to survive and make a personally-defined success of his life's work—without excessive suffering.

The remainder of this book comprises 19 concise chapters, each offering detailed advice and practical guidance on all essential aspects of successful career choice and job search for graduates and other qualified professionals.

o *Chapter 2* takes a closer took at the nature of careers in the last decade of the 20th century and explains how labour markets work in both theory and practice.

o *Chapter 3* invites you to enter the jobs jungle—a hostile environment, full of surprises for the unwary—and asks you to examine your own motivation and the kind of satisfaction you're seeking in employment.

o *Chapter 4* considers the ways in which you can start to help yourself in your career choice and job search—and suggests some external sources of help.

o *Chapter 5* stresses the importance of getting to know yourself, your more deeply felt personal needs and wants in employment, before you set out on your career choice and job search.

o *Chapter 6* offers practical advice on how to increase your self-confidence when setting out on your career. It encourages you to transform your negative fears and anxieties into a positive source of motivation and self-confidence—and offers explicit advice on how you should do this.

○ *Chapter 7* considers first how the majority of graduates will fare in their job search and early careers and then offers specific guidance to five groups who face special problems: older graduates; women; blacks and other ethnic minorities; gays and lesbians; and the disabled.

○ *Chapter 8* explains the distinction between finding a job and launching a career. It goes on to describe how to develop a relevant and effective career strategy as the next step towards launching yourself into a successful and rewarding career.

○ *Chapter 9* helps you to devise and implement appropriate tactics for your job search, comparing and contrasting traditional and innnovative tactics. It offers a list of practical suggestions on what to do when you still can't find the job you're after. It also introduces you to two powerful job search techniques, known respectively as 'Networking' and 'Cold Canvassing'.

○ *Chapter 10* seeks to demystify the entire recruitment and selection process, offering you a complete overview from the employer's perspective. It explains how employers set about the task of selecting the 'best' candidate, how you can increase your chances of being selected—and how to cope with interview rejection.

○ *Chapter 11* tells you how to read or 'decode' an employment advertisement. It goes on to offer detailed practical guidance on how you should set about completing a job application form and composing that critical accompanying letter of application.

○ *Chapter 12* explains the critical importance of a *curriculum vitae* (CV), perhaps the most important document you will ever prepare in your lifetime. There are several different forms of CV for use with different job applications. You are encouraged to think about the appropriate CV you may need when applying for different types of jobs.

○ *Chapter 13* takes a close look at the interview game, the rules by which the game is played, and suggests how to raise your game in order to emerge eventually as a winner. You can't learn to improve your interview technique simply by reading a book. But you'll need the advice we offer here before you can start to put it successfully into practice.

○ *Chapter 14* assumes you've been successful in securing your first offer of paid employment. It draws your attention to some of the legal pitfalls in negotiating your first contract of employment with specific advice on how to negotiate a better employment contract.

o *Chapter 15* continues with the theme of success by pointing out some of the ways in which you can make the most of your new appointment. It also indicates some of the risks and opportunities which now lie ahead of you in your new career. It provides a brief critical examination of State and employer pension plans and looks at a variety of ways in which you may wish to invest some of your newly-acquired disposable income.

o *Chapter 16* deals with vital aspects of occupational training, personal growth and career development. It introduces you to *The Self-Discovery Wheel*—a means of taking stock of your early career, helping you to discover whether you are fulfilling your major career aspirations or whether you need to seek further career guidance.

o *Chapter 17* analyses the reasons for employment appraisal and explains how organizations generally set about appraising their employees. It encourages you to explore the world of self-appraisal and offers suggestions on ways of improving your own job performance.

o *Chapter 18* invites you to consider whether you are a potential high flyer and offers some case studies of those who have demonstrated their high-flying skills. It also includes a dire warning to those who are tempted or pressurized into trying to fly too high, too soon.

o *Chapter 19* offers a variety of practical suggestions for promoting your early career and helping it prosper. We explain some proven ways of dealing with some typical early career crises and suggest ways in which you can make the most of a bad job by moving out—or moving on.

o *Chapter 20* briefly gathers together some of the main threads in this book, inviting you to reflect on on how far you've already come in your career—and to consider how far you still have to go.

If you're not yet ready to read the whole of this book before you embark on your career, keep it close by and read the relevant chapters in readiness for the challenges you will certainly face during the early years of your career.

*Good luck as you embark on your personal voyage of self-discovery and potential self-fulfilment—your own career choice and job search.*

# How careers and labour markets work

*I have put my genius into my life; all I've put into my work
is my talent.*

*Oscar Wilde, spoken to André Gide.*

André Gide: *Oscar Wilde: In Memoriam.*

Chapter 2 tries to do three things:

1. To explain how careers are now open to talent.
2. To distinguish work from paid employment.
3. To examine how labour markets work in theory and
   practice.

Historically, a career was not always a central life interest. The young have always pursued adventure, romance, glamour. It's true that in the three great medieval professions—law, medicine, and the Church—ambitious young men (but not young women) competed for relatively well-paid, demanding and prestigious jobs on some combined basis of qualification, merit and family or social connections.

The concept of a professional career, available to all those qualified for it—*the career open to talent*—is relatively modern. It dates from the French Revolution and from Napoleon himself. Perhaps there *were* a few soldiers in Napoleon's Grand Army naive enough to believe that every infantryman and fusilier carries a Field-Marshal's baton in his knapsack. Their hopes of a dazzling military career were invariably dashed—yet the Napoleonic ideal exercised an extraordinarily powerful and long-lasting effect on the minds of young men (and eventually young women) in Europe and indeed around the world. In place of qualification by birth, patronage or dynastic connection, the age of the new meritocracy had dawned. Whatever one's chosen field of employment—the army, the church, the law, the city—yes, even the Foreign Office, Ford Motor Company, Fortnum & Masons, or whatever—*energy and will-power* were henceforth regarded as the only essential pre-requisites for personal advancement and worldly success.

Through the example of Napoleon and his most successful lieutenants (no fewer than 16 of his 26 Marshals worked their way up through the ranks), a generation of ambitious young men (and perhaps a few young women) suddenly became aware that they could literally *take charge of their own lives* and *direct their careers* in ways totally inconceivable to their fathers and grandfathers before them. Throughout the 19th century, *energy and will-power*—in other words, qualification for social advancement and promotion through merit rather than through birth and family ties—held the keys to well-rewarded, high-status, satisfying careers.

The 20th century has built upon and vastly expanded the concept of 'Careers For All'. The combined effect of many factors, notably universal adult franchise, state-funded education and a greater measure of equal opportunity, now enable a far higher proportion of the working population to plan and develop rewarding and satisfying careers. This is not to gloss over the social injustice and frustration suffered by many in our society who are denied equal access to education and training, to jobs and promotion, and hence to satisfying, worthwhile careers. Racial, sexual and social discrimination persist in all the developed societies, both East and West. They cry out for urgent, critical investigation and correction.

Yet, as we enter the last decade before the second millenium, there's every reason to believe that the vast majority of college graduates will enjoy unprecedentedly successful careers, win glittering prizes through dazzling endeavour, scale new heights of ambition, derive immense satisfaction and reward from their work—yes, *and* serve their fellow men and women and their communities at the same time!

But let's be realistic. Not all will succeed. Not all will get to the top—or wish to do so. There will be casualties, too. None of us build worthwhile careers without some help and support. Nor should we forget those for whom the dream will fade or remain a dream, through some natural or social impediment. As we succeed, we should remember and care for them.

Those of us who succeed are not going to make it alone. *We need all the good advice and help we can muster.* In a terrifyingly competitive world, self-reliance is certainly a virtue. But every job hunter needs a network of contacts who will offer dispassionate advice, effect a useful introduction, suggest a name or provide a phone number. Every job hunter needs a close friend with whom she/he can talk through a tough career decision. Every job hunter needs a boss to whom she/he can turn for an honest yet supportive job reference. And we need to be available to support those who turn to us—for a letter of introduction or a reference, for therapeutic conversation, or simply a dry shoulder to cry on.

## WORK *versus* PAID EMPLOYMENT

At this point, we should make an important distinction between *useful work* and *paid employment*—both richly ambiguous terms in modern western society. According to the dictionary, work is 'what a person does—the result of one's labour—something accomplished'. Much of our life's work is *a labour of love*—work we delight in, work undertaken to benefit a person we love, work for which we neither receive nor expect any form of monetary compensation. A woman's work is never done. And for many a man whose occupation's gone, life loses its meaning, its central purpose. Asked how he felt after being sacked by Mrs Thatcher, following a 1985 Cabinet reshuffle, one former Government Minister gave this refreshingly frank and disarming reply:

The biggest effect on me was the hole in my life. From working 90 hours a week, I suddenly had nothing to do.[1]

But unlike millions of others who have lost their jobs through no fault of their own, at least *his* work represented *intrinsically satisfying and well-paid employment*. He doubtless received generous compensation. And soon found richly-rewarding alternative employment. Of that you may be sure.

By no means all of our work is paid employment. School children are give *home-work* by their teachers; university and college students often say they are *working hard* to pass their exams; many women in our society are now in *dual employment*—combining some form of generally *low-paid employment* in factory, shop or office with the domestic responsibility of *unpaid housework* and the raising of children.


## THE EMPLOYED, UNEMPLOYED AND SELF-EMPLOYED

*Employers and employees* are yoked together in a state of mutual dependence—even though that dependence is by no means equal. *Employees* need paid work to keep a roof over their heads and see their children fed. *Employers* are in business to produce goods and services, to make money, to be profitable. Because they need their workers' physical skills and mental abilities, they are willing to offer wages, salaries and other forms of direct or indirect remuneration to secure their employees' active co-operation or grudging subordination to superior authority.

*The unemployed*, by contrast, inhabit another country. For the vast majority of older men and women, brought up to believe that employment—rather than work—not only *is* but *should be* a central life interest, to be unemployed is to be outside society. Men made redundant frequently report feelings of impotence, of emasculation. Many women experience a massive sense of powerlessness—largely because they are so often treated as second-class citizens.

Millions of workers in Britain probably aspire to be *self-employed*, to run their own business and employ others. Many thousands set up in business every year on their own account; only hundreds succeed. *Self-employment* was probably never more popular amongst working men and women than it is today in Thatcherite Britain. But for the

[1] Lord Jenkin, formerly Patrick Jenkin: *The Daily Telegraph*, 24 July 1989.

vast majority of us, economic and personal survival probably still means a lifetime's useful labour spent in paid employment.

The future will almost certainly be different—periods of paid employment alternating with periods of unemployment and perhaps self-employment; periods of sabbatical leave for refreshment and re-qualification and with more frequent job and career changes; more unpaid voluntary work and much earlier retirement from paid employment for all. The traditional mould has been cracked if not yet completely shattered.

If we're lucky, we seek and find a good employer who will offer us—if not lifetime employment—then at least regular, reasonably paid, *full-time employment*. But in the past decade, there's been a vast upsurge in *part-time employment* so that today almost half of all women at work in Britain are in part-time employment. The length of the normal working week for full-time employees has already been reduced by one-third, from around 60 hours in 1900 (10 hours per day, six days per week) to around 40 hours at mid-century (8 hours per day, five days per week), and will probably be further cut to one-half at around 30 hours (7.5 hours per day, four days per week), by the end of the century.

In other words, although the world's work still calls out daily to be done, we live in an age of growing leisure and increasing affluence—with all the personal and social problems which they bring: from obesity to endemic heart disease; from the convenient, throwaway aerosol to the greenhouse effect; from the two-car family to acid rain; from more equal employment opportunities to yuppie-style, premature burn-out.

In terms of paid employment, there was surely never before a time when school-leavers and graduates have faced such a fascinating diversity of career opportunities and of rewarding jobs to be done. In little more than a century of accelerating scientific and technological innovation, we've come from rural poverty and urban destitution to vast agricultural surpluses; from dispersed handicraft production to capital-intensive, high-technology robotics. And yet every one of these technological and commercial advances has opened up the alluring prospect of exciting new career choices and fresh job opportunities!

## HOW LABOUR MARKETS WORK IN THEORY AND PRACTICE

How will traditional labour markets accommodate the shifting patterns of supply and demand for the more highly-skilled workforce which these new industries require? Let's begin with a simplified theoretical model of markets before examining the distinctive features of specific labour markets.

The market-place is the focal point—the very heart—of most human communities the world over. As an intellectual concept and as a human artifact, the market fulfils a variety of useful functions, both latent and manifest, for those capable of recognizing and exploiting them:

- It is a *physical meeting place* for traders—buyers and sellers of goods and services—to haggle and bargain over the terms of exchange in every kind of national and international currency.

- It is an *economic mechanism* for allocating scarce resources by bringing supply and demand into some kind of equilibrium, despite all kinds of dislocations and distortions.

- It is a *symbolic device*, representing the primacy of economics over morality and ideology in both capitalist and social-market economies— from New York, Tokyo and London to Warsaw, Moscow and now even Beijing.

Despite superficial differences in their structure, location and content, all markets share a number of common features and functions. In all essentials, a *labour market* is no different from a stock-market—short- horned or gilt-edged—except that:

- *Human labour* normally has a better sense of its own *market capacity* or *economic value* than do beef cattle or junk bonds, and therefore retains some responsibility for settling the terms on which it is willing to trade.

- *Human labour* represents a different *ethical category* from either beef cattle or junk bonds—i.e. people should never be treated as merely the means to other people's ends but as ends in themselves.

In theory, a labour market is made up of myriad pairs of buyers and sellers who enter the market because each potential trader has something of relative scarcity value to trade against some equally valuable asset owned by another trader. As traders acquire information about who's who and what's what 'in the market' on a particular day, they build up a mental picture—a data base, a particular kind of 'knowledge' of that market—or a specialized corner of that market. In the case of labour markets, traders soon discover the 'going rate'—

i.e. the currently prevailing parity or rate of exchange for various specified categories of labour.

When trading begins, pairs of buyers and sellers will haggle or negotiate over these rates of exchange until they arrive at a mutually agreeable 'price' for some particular category of labour. The negotiating or bargaining process itself is made up of an exceedingly subtle, complex and elusive set of physical and psychological transactions. The negotiators move incrementally away from their initially irreconcilable bargaining positions towards an equilibrium point at which, though neither achieves all of his bargaining objectives, each achieves sufficient of those objectives to make possible some compromise settlement.

Traders who reach such a settlement by 'striking a bargain' often signify their agreement in a symbolic act—such as the shaking of hands or the drinking of a toast, or the signing of a document, usually the employment contract. This document constitutes a legally binding agreement which specifies the terms of the economic bargain which has just been struck and the economic exchange with follows thereafter.

To observe the workings of a labour market in a traditional agrarian society, we need go no further than our own local village in early spring when shepherds hire themselves out to tenant farmers for the lambing season; or in the autumn, when agricultural labourers hire themselves out to farmers to bring home the harvest. For those without easy access to a local village where these traditional hiring practices take place, there are a number of vivid literary descriptions of these agricultural 'hiring fairs' as they are known in the novels of Thomas Hardy.[2]

In modern, industrial society, the same hiring function often takes place amongst industrial workers through an intermediate agency, once known as a local *labour exchange* now universally referred to in Britain as a *Job Centre* or *Job Shop*. More highly skilled or qualified workers may seek employment through the *Professional and Executive Register*; or through some other commercial employment agency; or by simply responding to one of the many paid advertisements placed in certain so-called 'quality' newspapers and magazines, whose specialized pages are dedicated to this lucrative match-making business.

Labour markets operate at different geographical levels through an increasingly wider range of orbits:

- *Local labour markets* operate within the relatively small radius of a given city or town centre (e.g. London, Birmingham or Glasgow) and

[2] See, *inter alia*, Thomas Hardy: *Far From the Madding Crowd*.

cater for the needs of employers and workers who choose to operate within that radius.

- *Regional labour markets* operate within a much wider radius of some more broadly-defined geographical area (e.g. London and the South East of England; Merseyside; the South-West) and cater for the needs of those within that radius.

- *National labour markets* operate within the borders of a given nation state (e.g. the British or French or German labour market) and cater for the nationals of that state plus those foreign nationals and foreign-based organizations which have secured legal rights to operate within the borders of another state (e.g. Nissan in Britain or ICI in the United States).

- *International labour markets* operate across national frontiers and cater for the needs of those who are legally entitled to pursue careers anywhere in the 'free' world.

Each of these labour markets may be further sub-divided or segmented to cater for specific groups of employers and workers (e.g. the Glasgow market for unskilled labour; or the labour market for skilled electrical maintenance workers in London and the South East; or the international market for high-calibre economics graduates).

Labour markets vary greatly in the extent to which they are 'open' or 'closed' to new entrants. For example, entry to the already overcrowded London market for theatrical talent is open only to members of Equity, the dominant trade union operating in the entertainment industry. Conversely, the British motor industry operates in a relatively open market which encourages the entry of foreign motor manufacturers, several of whom have now set up in this country, as well as the migration of workers from one part of Britain to another to take advantage of whatever job opportunities these investments may offer. The fewer the restrictions on entry, the less the degree of fragmentation or segmentation within the labour market, the greater the shared knowledge amongst would-be traders, the more competitive the market.

From these broad definitions, it's not difficult to see why those graduates or others who seek paid employment will find it very much more difficult to break into certain labour markets than into others. For example, it's impossible for qualified medical graduates to enter the national market for medical practitioners in Britain unless they already belong to the British Medical Association, the professional body which organizes and represents doctors in Britain. Conversely, almost any graduate may obtain entry to the British market for business executives—although women still find the upper echelons of that particular market much less open to them, due to sex discrimination and gender prejudice.

## WHO LAUNCHES A WORTHWHILE CAREER IN THE 1990s?

It should now be clear, from what has been said in this chapter that, amongst those who succeed in launching themselves into the most worthwhile careers over the next decade, there will be a very large number of graduates and others with professional qualifications. Recent research in Britain, the United States and elsewhere shows conclusively that the most satisfying, worthwhile, rewarding and secure jobs always go to the most highly qualified, younger members of society. More specifically, the best jobs go to those amongst the most highly qualified who have devised *a successful career strategy* which they have been able to implement by means of a *purposeful job search* and who demonstrate the most intelligent handling of *job applications* and of *interview techniques.* Those who *fail* to launch successful careers—despite having good paper qualifications—invariably include those who have neglected these vital steps in career choice and job search and have therefore *failed to take charge of their own lives and their own careers. To launch a successful career and obtain a worthwhile job means doing your homework properly.*

### SUGGESTIONS FOR FURTHER READING

E. H. Schein: *Career Dynamics: Matching Individual and Organizational Needs,* Reading MA: Addison-Wesley (1971).

Charles Handy: *The Future of Work*, Oxford: Blackwell (1984).

Richard Pearson: 'Graduate Employment Trends' in *GO: Graduate Opportunities,* London: Newpoint Publishing Co. (1987).

P. Herriot: *Down from the Ivory Tower: Graduates and Their Jobs,* Chichester: Wiley (1984).

M. Adams and P. Meadows: 'The changing graduate labour market' *Department of Employment Gazette.* Vol 93, No 9, pp 343–91.

Richard Pearson and Kenneth Walsh: *How to analyze your local labour market,* Aldershot: Gower (1983).

# The jobs jungle: How hungry are you?

*There are two things to aim at in life: first, to get what you want; and, after that, to enjoy it. Only the wisest of mankind achieve the second.*

Logan Pearsall Smith (1867–1961): *Afterthoughts*

Chapter 3 tries to do three things:

1. To reconnoitre the jobs jungle facing job hunters.
2. To discover what most job hunters are after.
3. To probe the meaning of motivation and job satisfaction.

In his romantic mind's eye, the author sees job hunters as youthful explorers venturing for the first time into the jobs jungle—mysterious yet hauntingly beautiful. Each explorer hacks his way through the treacherous undergrowth, in competitive pursuit of some uniquely exotic species. To ensure the success of such a hunting expedition, job hunters need to be alert and eagle-eyed, highly motivated and properly trained. They must be capable of deploying all their skills and experience if they are to track down, capture and bring home that most elusive of quarries—let's call it *job satisfaction.*

Over the top? Perhaps. But remember this: if you don't survive in the jobs jungle, you're not going to eat. The jobs jungle can be a lonely place, a hostile environment, full of unpleasant surprises for the unwary. Of course, like all quests, job hunting can be exciting. Adrenalin courses through the blood. Your enthusiasm may easily run away with you, leading you astray. In the end, you're out there alone. You may encounter frustration, disappointment, even despair. You suddenly catch a glimpse of what appears to be your quarry—only to discover that it's an illusion. Even when your quarry seems within your grasp, it may still slip away—and you must begin the search all over again.

Before you set out for the jobs jungle, it pays to take careful stock of your resources and to inoculate yourself against disappointment. *The crucial questions are these:*

- How hungry are you?

- How strong is your motivation, your commitment, your will to succeed?

- Can you summon the necessary energy, sustain the tough pace, meet the intense competition, handle the painful rejection?

- Have you the stamina to keep going until you fulfil your ambition, achieve your career goals?

- Most importantly, are you sure you know what it is you're seeking?

## WHAT ARE MOST JOB HUNTERS AFTER?

We begin with a paradox: that whilst *we are all unequal*—in physical and mental gifts, in appearance and temperament, in interests and aptitudes, in tastes and preferences, in goals and aspirations—there is nevertheless a sense in which *we may claim to be, or be deemed to be, equal*—for example, in our claim to equal consideration for a share of the good things of life, to equal treatment before the law, to equal job opportunities. *Even, perhaps, to equal job satisfaction.*

When it comes to career choice and job search, whatever their chosen profession or field of employment, *all job hunters are hungry for much the same kinds of things*, however differently they define their job satisfaction or express their personal career needs and wants.

## ARE YOU AS HUNGRY AS A HUNTER?

*How many items on this check list represent what you want from employment?*

1. *Intellectual stimulation* of a kind and level in keeping with your mental capacity to perform your work without undue stress.

2. A mixture of *regular activities* coupled with *periodic challenge and variety.*

3. A *sense of achievement*, recognition for having accomplished something inherently worthwhile, not merely trivial but of enduring value.

4. Adequate *financial or material rewards* or recompense for your labour time with some differential compensation to reflect the relative worth of any special skill you possess or special contribution you may make.

5. *Good working conditions*, in line with legislated standards or current best practice in terms of environmental health and safety.

6. *Congenial colleagues* with whom you may share some sense of community, of joint achievement, of solidarity.

7. The opportunity to be periodically stretched to your limits for *personal growth and development of your human potentiality*, to become your 'best self'.

8. The chance to be considered for *promotion or advancement* to more demanding, more responsible, better–paid work for which you may be qualified.

9. The opportunity *to exercise responsibility* and, by doing so successfully, to occupy roles of increasing trust and discretion.

10. *Autonomy*, the freedom to take responsible action without close instruction or supervision.

# JOB SATISFACTION AND MOTIVATION

We have been reluctant to use the blanket term '*job satisfaction*' because it masks a multitude of subtle, subjective feelings about employment wants and needs which deserve more detailed exploration. For a long time, *job satisfaction and dissatisfaction* were thought to represent opposite ends of one continuous spectrum of a common work experience. If we experienced *dissatisfaction at work*, it was thought to be due to the absence of something mysterious called 'job satisfaction'. Conversely, if we experienced the warm glow of *job satisfaction*, then that 'mysterious something' was manifestly present in our work. The terms were thus interconnected and antithetical.

## MASLOW'S MOTIVATIONAL THEORY OF HIERARCHICAL NEEDS

Early writers on human motivation based their theories on the common observation that most people respond to two primary instinctual drives:

- *To maximize pleasure* (i.e. a positive inducement in the form of some reward or encouragement).

- *To minimize pain* (i.e. a negative inducement in the form of some punishment or withholding of a material or non-material benefit).

This somewhat crude 'carrot and stick' theory of human motivation held sway for several centuries until a more sophisticated modern theory of human behaviour emerged to explain the limits of human motivation (e.g. why some employees are evidently less responsive to certain kinds of inducement than other employees).

Building on the work of earlier academic researchers, an American psychologist, Abraham Maslow, first advanced in 1954 what has probably become the best-known modern explanation of the linkages between work content, motivation, job satisfaction and job performance. In essence, Maslow argued that, in every aspect of our lives, we always act in ways which seek to fulfil our subjectively-defined needs.

The central thrust of Maslow's theory is this:

- That we cannot fulfil our higher order needs unless and until our lower order needs have first been met.

- That once a lower order need has been met, it ceases to be a motivator and we then seek to fulfil a higher order need.

- That once we achieve the fulfilment of our most powerful, highest order needs, our motivation becomes self-sustaining and no further external stimulus or motivation is needed.

These needs are arranged in a steeply ascending hierarchy:

**Highest**
**self-actualization needs**
*Continued self-development and personal*
*fulfilment of one's human potentiality.*

**Higher esteem needs**
*Achievement, status, recognition.*

**Safety and social needs**
*Shelter, belonging, friendship, love.*

**Basic physiological or survival needs**
*Oxygen, food, water, sex.*

## RELEVANCE OF MASLOW'S THEORY TO CAREER CHOICE AND JOB SEARCH

Maslow's theory of motivation has direct relevance in the context of career choice and job search. In seeking our first paid employment we're unlikely to be primarily concerned with abstract notions of job satisfaction. Understandably enough, this may lead us to accept the highest-paid job offer we receive, regardless of its longer-term career possibilities.

Thereafter, we're likely to make several job changes in our mid-twenties in order to achieve ever-higher financial or material rewards. In our first years of employment, we're preoccupied with meeting our basic needs (i.e. sufficient salary to buy and furnish a home, to enjoy spending on material items like a car, clothes, holidays, etc.). Once we achieve a certain level of salary (i.e. sufficient to accumulate some savings, after meeting regular domestic expenditures), our motivation shifts towards meeting some of our higher order needs (i.e. recognition and status). In time, having achieved some self-defined level of seniority and promotion within the hierarchy (e.g. first-line management), salary and status cease to be the prime motivators and we turn our attention to meeting some of our higher order needs (e.g. creativity, self-esteem, self-development, self-fulfilment).

Maslow seems to offer a powerfully persuasive theory which helps to explain the behaviour of many job hunters in the early years of their careers. Objections may nevertheless be raised from several directions. Feminists might argue, for example, that Maslow's model fits stereotypical male career profiles better than female profiles because women's fulfilment of their higher order needs is often frustrated by gender discrimination and sometimes compensated by their acceptance of maternal and family responsibilities. One response to this might be that, where higher order needs are not met within the work context, they may be sought by both men and women outside their working lives.

## HERZBERG MODIFIES MASLOW

The work of Frederick Herzberg, another American industrial psychologist, has substantially modified our acceptance of Maslow's work. From the mid-1960s Herzberg began to teach that, far from being at opposite ends of the same subjectively felt hierarchy of needs, the terms '*job satisfaction*' and '*job dissatisfaction*' refer to vastly different kinds of human experience. '*Job dissatisfaction*', argues Herzberg, is obviously important because it restricts or inhibits our work performance—in the same way that the lack of adequate health and safety affects us by its failure to provide *a hygienic working environment*. The kinds of things which make us feel dissatisfied, says Herzberg, are low pay, poor working conditions, inadequate fringe benefits, and so on. As soon as any of these dissatisfactions are remedied—for example, by a pay rise, an improvement in working conditions or fringe benefits—we find we're dissatisfied again shortly afterwards. *In other words, job dissatisfaction keeps recurring, like hunger, thirst or the sex drive.* There is thus no way in which improved 'hygiene' can ever satisfy us. '*Job satisfaction*' is quite different. It refers *not to hygiene factors but to genuine motivators*—like challenging work content, an inherent sense of achievement, of psychological growth fostered by encouragement and recognition by one's boss.

As employees, we may put pressure on our employers to reduce our job dissatisfaction, by providing a safer and healthier working environment. If they fail to meet such demands, we may well seek to change our employer—but still experience job dissatisfaction and fail to find genuine job satisfaction. For *what employees really yearn for is not simply more money but increased job satisfaction—something which all too many employers fail to provide*. Because every individual is different, we all seek different forms of job satisfaction—yet we all acknowledge that its achievement is of paramount importance to us in our careers and our daily work.

## RECENT MOTIVATION THEORY

Finally, there are the more recent *expectancy–valency theories* associated with the names of Vroom, Lawler and Porter. They argue that:

- Every individual has different goals/aspirations.

- Individuals only exert themselves to achieve those goals if they believe there is a reasonable expectation that effort leads to achievement.

- Individual motivation therefore depends on the valency (or value) placed on those goals/aspirations.

Expectancy–valency theories have important implications for employee motivation and performance because they move away from the general mass and closer to the individual, where all true motivation occurs. In short, when it comes down to career choice and job search, we are dealing with some of the most obscure areas of human motivation. Indeed, there are many successful careerists who are unable to explain precisely what it is that motivates them to be so successful in their chosen occupations.

It pays to think carefully about your own personal goals/aspirations before you set out into the jobs jungle. Your successful expedition into the jobs jungle depends very largely on your knowing the nature of the quarry you seek to capture and bring home.

## SUGGESTIONS FOR FURTHER READING

E. D. Deci: *Intrinsic Motivation*, New York: Plenum (1975).

F. Herzberg: *Work and The Nature of Man*, London: Staples Press (1968).

F. Herzberg: 'One more time: how do you motivate employees?', *Harvard Business Review*, Vol 33 pp 53–62 (1971).

E. E. Lawler and L. W. Porter: *Managerial Attitudes and Performance*, Chicago: Irwin Dorsey (1968).

A. H. Maslow: *Motivation and Personality*. New York: Harper & Bros. (1954).

A. H. Maslow: 'A theory of human motivation', *Psychological Review*. Vol 50, pp 370–396. (1943).

V. H. Vroom: *Work and Motivation*. Chichester: John Wiley (1964).

# chapter 4

# Where to start looking for help

*Help me if you can, I'm feeling down,*
*And I do appreciate you being around.*
*Help me get my feet back on the ground.*
*Won't you please, please help me?*

The Beatles (1965)

Chapter 4 tries to do three things:

1. To explore the limits of self-help.
2. To review some external sources of help.
3. To suggest what you can do to help yourself.

## YOU'RE NEVER ALONE WITH A PROBLEM—OR ARE YOU?

When you've finished college but seem unable to make that critical breakthrough into your chosen career, do you feel entirely alone, struggling with an insoluble problem? If so, consider the man at the centre of the Ridley Melt-Down Crisis:

### THE RIDLEY MELT-DOWN CRISIS

*It's 2 a.m. and you're alone in Central Control at the newly-privatized Ridley Atomic Power Corporation. (How you came to be there is another matter.) The fact is, you're alone—completely alone, now. What's more, you're locked in. Your friend Paddy Moneghan, Ridley's Chief Security Guard, who let you into Central Control on perfectly legitimate business, just over two hours ago, lies crumpled at your feet. Three times he's failed to respond to your enthusiastic kiss of life. You've repeatedly dialled 999 to get help—a doctor, the police, anybody—but the line's completely dead. Like poor Paddy, there. Nothing more he can do for you—or you for him. Probably myocardial infarction.*

*Your attention refocuses on that brain-piercing klaxon that's been screaming for what seems like hours from the overhead loudspeakers. And that sinister blood-red light, endlessly pulsing over the control panel. You fling yourself into the Controller's chair, frantically scanning the console dials, levers, on–off switches. Some of them already seem incandescent: gas pressure—1097; core temperature—over 2500 and rising; cooling water temperature—zero. The fail-safe button's knocked into the OUT position, damn it! Seventeen other lights/hooters flashing/screaming for attention. Where to start? The digital clock blinks 02.17. Next shift due on at 06.00. Almost four hours away. Yes. You're alone all right! And the reactor core's just minutes away from total melt-down. You're trapped. You know you can't get out. And you know you can't bring help in. Even with all Paddy's keys...*

What you do in the next few minutes will decide not merely your own personal future—but that of the rest of Southern Britain...All that separates Western Europe from an assured nuclear winter now is your creative thinking...

Relax! It's only a 'warm-up' exercise in problem solving and creative thinking (see end of chapter for possible answers). But it serves to focus attention on the helplessness and isolation we all feel at some time in our lives. Although men and women are social animals (we weren't made for society, society was made for us) it often seems we're utterly alone with our problems. What *can* we do in such circumstances to help ourselves? Where do we summon up the energy, the will-power, the courage to keep going, to call up outside help—without which we feel we may not survive?

Take career choice and job search, for example. We survived college and made it through finals alone... well, with a little help from family and friends, teachers and tutors, advisors and study counsellors, landlady and bank manager. So, why do we need help now, when we've finished college and stand on the very brink of our working lives, ready to take the plunge into our unknown careers?

Perhaps we're reluctant to admit it—because it saps our self-confidence, undermines our self-reliance, questions our self-sufficiency. But the fact is probably this—that most of us go through life needing help throughout the whole perilous mission—from the womb to the tomb. As infants, we're totally dependent. As children we're being continually watched and protected from self-destruction. As adolescents we're allowed to make our own mistakes—sometimes with ghastly consequences. As mature adults, we're constantly turning to professional advisors, counsellors, consultants, therapists. Finally, in old age, we settle down into the dotage of 'learned helplessness'. In short, it's doubtful whether we achieve any single worthwhile thing alone and entirely unaided. Without all that technical back-up and moral support—which we take for granted and so rarely acknowledge—where would we be?

So, when it comes to career choice and job search, we have to admit we've no real freedom of action: our choice of future career is heavily influenced—perhaps even decisively determined—by external forces: by parental and grand-parental expectations; by peer-group pressure; by coming under the spell of some leading charismatic figure—Laurence Olivier, Mother Theresa, Oliver North, Eddie the Eagle, Edwina Currie, Robbie Coltrane, Ben Elton, whoever.

## Mark's story

Eldest of five brothers and three sisters, Mark was probably as intellectually gifted as any of his siblings, two of whom went to Cambridge and achieved the highest academic honours. Yet Mark was destined for his father's workshop at age 14 and earned his living with carpenter's tools for the first half of his half-fulfilled life. Except for two wartime years when he became sergeant in the Intelligence Corps, teaching mathematics to rookies during initial training.

Never more fully at home than when arguing the unpopular side ▶ of any moral or political issue, Mark was as well-read as a radically-minded professor. Nevertheless, he made the grievous error of setting up in a small way of business with two members of his family. They spent more time and energy disagreeing amongst themselves than in making money. So the business flopped.

Mark made up for his own lack of formal schooling by encouraging all three of his own children to go to university. Each of them went on to build a distinguished professional career; Dominic, the eldest, is a top computer specialist; Henrietta, the second, teaches philosophy at Cambridge; Albert, the third, is in demand as a management consultant.

Mark was proud of all three of his children. They may even have offered some consolation for his own career frustration. After hearing his funeral eulogy, some of us asked this question: What might his life have been, if he'd managed to reach Cambridge himself? Read, mark and learn!

## WHERE DO WE TURN FOR HELP?

Not to acquaintances, with whom we pass the time of day, but to a particular member of the family—or a trusted friend, perhaps, with whom, if we're lucky enough, we talk the sun down and wear the night out with conversation. A friend is someone with whom you can share thoughts and feelings you'd never share with your mother. A friend can tell you you're overweight, have bad breath or need a bath—and still remain your friend. We all need encouragement. But we also need somebody to tell us, quite simply, that we're not going to make it—that we simply haven't the diaphragm control for Covent Garden, the killer instinct for Wimbledon, or the visceral qualities for Number 10. So, it's back to the career drawing board.

After family and friends probably come career counselling agencies, commercial or professional. If you're wise, you'll have already been in touch with your University Appointments Board or your Careers Advisory Service—often staffed with very helpful people. Except that they see hundreds of others and, rather like overworked General Medical Practitioners—seem ready to prescribe without always devoting sufficient time to the diagnosis. In any case, the queues for everything on campus seem interminable.

The Careers Service, run by your local regional council, has a statutory duty to provide career guidance for school-leavers, but may also be willing to see adults (whether graduates, professionals or otherwise) by appointment. You will normally be given the opportunity to take one of several computer-based vocational interest test programmes—such as JIGCAL (Job Ideas and Information Generator—Computer Assisted Learning) designed for school-leavers or CASCAID (Careers Advisory Service Computer Aid) designed for a more academic and older age-group. In addition to receiving detailed information on the career field of your choice, you may also be offered what is called 'in-depth vocational guidance'. It's worth pointing out that the service is free and that Careers Officers are usually highly sympathetic because they are themselves graduates and therefore understand the pressures you are under to find a suitable job.

By contrast, commercial agencies tend to be slick and expensive. They'll put you through whole batteries of special aptitude, psychological or psychometric tests—then offer you advice on the basis of their own interpretation of your scores, correct to three places of decimals. Their fees may range from £300 to £3000. And you may think the money well spent—if they succeed in persuading you not to become a concert pianist or a tightrope walker, a chiropodist or an actuary.

There are generally two types of commercial employment agencies:

- Those which simply offer career counselling, advice and guidance, based on some form of diagnostic interview, testing or other form of investigation.

- Those which go beyond advice and guidance and which, for a further substantial fee, will advise you of job vacancies and send you weekly lists of selected or unselected vacancies.

Until we have more scientific evidence to substantiate their claims, we should probably steer clear of phrenologists, graphologists and crystal-ball gazers.

Then there are Government agencies. Surely they're bound to be worth a visit—especially since they're free? It's precisely because their services *are* free that Job Centre staff are processing hundreds or perhaps thousands of client applications at any one time. You may strike lucky. Or, conversely, you may find they're all members of NALGO, out on strike for more money and better working conditions, which they justly deserve. They may not make you feel your welfare is their prime concern. Let's face it, they're not in very well-paid jobs themselves.

By now, you may begin to feel a bit depressed and sorry for yourself—especially if most of your peers seem to be getting interviews or landing job offers. What's to be done? There's clearly a limit to the number of friends who still have dry padded shoulders to weep on. There may be hints that you've already become a nuisance at home, or in your digs. Especially if you're not paying your way.

## WHAT EXACTLY IS YOUR PROBLEM?

Let's begin by distinguishing between:

- **1.** *Those without a clue where to start*—because they've been concentrating on their academic work, or a love affair, or the college drama society, or working late nights in a local hostelry or restaurant to make enough money to help keep body and mortar board together.

- **2.** *Those still unsure about their career choice*; or who describe themselves as 'very open minded'—meaning they're not committed but are willing to look at any job vacancy on its merits.

- **3.** *Those who despair of getting an interview*, despite the fact that they know very clearly which career they wish to pursue, but don't seem to be able to land an interview, let alone a job offer.

- **4.** *Those who never receive a single job offer*, despite feeling they've done well at interview.


○ **(1)** *above: For those without a clue where to start.* You've got to move fast, get down to the library and do some rapid relevant reading. There are several excellent publications, offering both generalized and special advice, well worth reading, on where to start your career choice and job search:


— *GO (Graduate Opportunities)*—the self-proclaimed 'leading employment directory', which runs to more than 1000 pages, including much glossy paid advertising. It's published annually around March by the Newpoint Publishing Company, London, publishers of the Directory of Graduate Guides, *Graduate Post* and a wide range of employment and educational titles. It's distributed free throughout the UK. It even carries an endorsement from the Secretary of State for Education who writes in the following anodyne terms:

> I am sure this [umpteenth] edition of GO will provide a useful source of reference and advice for final year students.

— *GET (the annual guide to Graduate Employment and Training* plus the Graduate studies supplement) is published by the Careers Research and Advisory Centre (CRAC), a non-profit-making body, founded in 1964. Working entirely in the field of careers education, CRAC's aim is to create links between the world of education and employment and, in particular, to help graduates, school-leavers and the qualified with their career decisions. CRAC materials are produced, marketed and sold under exclusive licence by Hobsons Limited, Cambridge.

○ *(2) above: For those uncertain about their careers.* We suggest you lose no time in reading Chapters 5, 8 and 9 below.

○ *(3) above: For those who despair of getting an interview.* We suggest you proceed immediately to Chapters 9, 10 and 11 below.

○ *(4) above: For those who never receive a single job offer.* We recommend that you pay close attention to the advice given in Chapter 13 below.

*Whichever of the above categories* you may be in, we also strongly recommend you to read Chapter 9 and to *learn all you can about Networking and Cold Canvassing.*

## SOME IDEAS FOR HANDLING THE RIDLEY MELT-DOWN CRISIS
What can you do when all seems lost? So long as you have electric light (or a torch), you can still read. The switches on most consoles are labelled ON/OFF. They can be moved singly or in combination. Levers can be moved from side to side, pushed or pulled, and the results observed. Critical valves are often painted red and can be turned anti-clockwise/clockwise to OPEN/SHUT (or vice versa). By trial and error you may well be able to shut down the entire system without risking an explosion. Think of it this way: What have you possibly got to lose by experimentation at this stage? You've everything to play for and every opportunity to think and act swiftly. And the best of British luck!

## SUGGESTIONS FOR FURTHER READING
Richard N. Bolles: *What Color Is Your Parachute? A Practical Manual for Job-Hunters and Career Changers*, Berkeley CA: Ten Speed Press (1987 and annual).

Gill Cox and Sheila Dainow: *Making The Most of Yourself*, London: Sheldon Press (1985).

Richard Nelson-Jones: *Human Relations Skills: Training in Self-Help*, Eastbourne: Cassell Education (1986).

# How well do you know yourself?

*La plus grande chose du monde, c'est de savoir être à soi.*
*(The most important thing in the world is to know how to*
*be one's self.)*

Montaigne (1533–1592): *Essays*

Chapter 5 tries to do three things:

1. To stress the importance of self-knowledge in career choice.
2. To probe the meaning of self-knowledge.
3. To suggest ways to deepen self-knowledge and to develop a better understanding of your career needs.

Sir Thomas Beecham, brilliant orchestral conductor and scabrous wit, said one should try everything in life once—except incest and Morris Dancing. For most of us, alas, life is too short to try more than a limited range of the potential experiences which it offers. When it comes to careers, for example, many of us settle for just one. The question is: Which one?

How many of us are lucky enough when young to know for certain what our future career will be? When Laurence Olivier—arguably Britain's most distinguished actor—died in July 1989, BBC TV screened an interview recorded some 20 years earlier in which Olivier, then at the height of his powers, talked to drama critic Kenneth Tynan about his early life and subsequent career. Asked how early in life he discovered that he wanted to become an actor, Olivier replied that, although he had greatly enjoyed taking various roles in school plays, he had never given much serious thought before then to his future career. Then, one day, he and his family travelled to Tilbury, where his much-loved older brother was about to embark for India to become a tea planter. Olivier recalled how, on his tearful way home, he had turned to his father, a Church of England Minister, and asked how soon he, too, could become a tea planter and follow his brother to India. To his amazement, his father immediately responded by saying that—far from following in his brother's footsteps—young Laurence was destined for the stage. From that moment on, said Olivier, he knew that his entire life would be bound up with the theatre.

'And what do *you* intend to be when you leave school?' Most of us recall being repeatedly asked that fatuous question by importunate relatives and friends of the family. A handful of exceptional youngsters—who have had their palms read or correctly construed the plum stones—may well respond to some inner voice—a prompting, a calling—telling them to pursue some specific vocation—tinker, tailor, soldier, sailor, doctor, minister or missionary perhaps. Frankly, most of us haven't the faintest idea what career path we intend to pursue as adults. How can we be expected to know, at the age of 8 or 18, what it means in practice to be a Consultant Venereologist, or a Junk Bond Dealer, or a Leader Writer on *The Independent*, or Audit Trail Executive with an International Blue Chip Credit Card Corporation? We can hardly understand—let alone provide a worthwhile answer to—that familiar, fatuous question!

By the time we reach college or university, most of us may have some romantic, vague notions about possible careers. We shall certainly not follow Daddy into the Church of England—or the BBC, or the whelk stall. But should we perhaps follow in big brother's (or sister's?) footsteps by becoming a Tea Planter (do they still exist?) or a Psychiatrist, Computer Programmer, Fashion Designer, Airline Pilot or whatever?

We simply don't know. And the reason is perfectly simple: like most undergraduates we still lack two critically important sets of knowledge: (a) *knowledge about ourselves*; and (b) *knowledge about possible careers*. For example:

*(a)* Who am I?
How do I want to spend my working life?
What am I likely to be any good at?
What satisfactions and frustrations may I expect?
Am I likely to stay in one career for most of my life?

*(b)* What does a Solicitor actually do?
How much does a BBC Producer earn?
Where do you start if you want to become a Missionary?
If I want to become a Psychiatrist, must I first qualify as a Physician?

As we grow older, we begin to understand what Kirkegaard meant when he said that life is lived forwards, but understood backwards. At 15, a girl may be convinced she intends to be a ballet dancer (or, failing that, a Newmarket jockey). At 18, she may concede that she hasn't the talent for the stage, or the physical stamina for the turf. Her earlier ambitions may have been unrealistic but she may still not know what she *really* wants to do with her life. By the time she's 22 and has graduated with a respectable BA Degree in Business Studies, she may gladly settle for a well-paid and intellectually demanding job in the Central Marketing Division of Unilever or ICI, based in Bristol or Basle or British Columbia. By the time she's 30, she may have discovered precisely what she wants to do with the rest of her life— after taking a career break to raise a family!

## WHAT DOES SELF-KNOWLEDGE MEAN?

Although teenagers are supposed to be excessively self-absorbed, most of us complete up to four years at college without devoting much time to thinking critically and constructively about ourselves or our possible careers. We did not ask to be born. But we're not yet ready to die. How then should we occupy the interval in a sensible and enjoyable way?

The ancient world struggled long and hard with these philosophical conundrums. The ancient Greeks made a good start. They concluded that, since man was the measure of all things, we must identify and develop our physical, intellectual and moral capacities to their limits. In this process of self-discovery, knowledge of all kinds—and more especially self-knowledge—was a distinctive kind of virtue.

The Jewish people, by contrast, were given the Mosaic Code (the Ten Commandments) to live by. But the Code fell short of offering advanced career counselling to an essentially nomadic, pastoral people. Christianity added two supremely difficult injunctions: that we should also love our enemies; and that we should make the fullest possible best use of any God-given talent. Once again, self-knowledge is at the heart of the mystery. Our self-development and human fulfilment depend upon our discovering and coming to terms with our natural gifts, our acquired skills and our limitations—and putting them to work for the benefit of the community. Thus the Christian work ethic was born.

From the Renaissance onwards, man has been repeatedly called upon to apply more consistent scientific analysis to identifying and then being true to his own distinctive nature:

This above all, to thine own self be true
And it must follow as the night the day
Thou cans't not then be false to any man.

William Shakespeare: *Hamlet*

In more modern times, philosophers and psychologists, poets and playwrights have taught us that, whilst we have many 'selves', we have a moral obligation to become the 'best self' of which we are capable. To be fully human is to be stretched to the limits of our capacities—to be all we can be. In short, we live under the continuous obligation to grow in physical, intellectual, spiritual and moral stature; to develop our skills, interests and talents to the utmost; and to fulfil ourselves as best we may in our brief lives.

In more prosaic terms, to make the most of our lives we need to understand and come to terms with the self. But what is the self? Many of us experience an identity crisis in our late teens or early twenties, struggling to come to terms with the complex concepts and experiences of 'self' which are loaded with rich ambiguities, paradoxes and meanings.

Modern psychology urges us to get to know ourselves better by exploring this multi-dimensional web of relationships; by observing nature; by a close reading of significant literature; by field investigation of social issues; by artistic creativity; by keeping a personal journal;

by preparing a family history; and so on. Some of the richest opportunities we are afforded to confront and get to know ourselves derive from those periodic crises which punctuate our human existence: bereavement, loss, grief, sickness, death, divorce, redundancy, rejection, etc.

Getting to know ourselves is not easy. It requires sustained effort, patience, courage and imagination. Nevertheless, if we want to know where we're going, we need a much clearer idea where we're coming from. Even this modest degree of self-knowledge is not attainable without a great deal of unaccustomed, even painful, introspection.

At the most basic level, do we have any realistic idea what physical impression we make on other people? Could we provide a reasonably accurate and coherent account of how we look—say, when we arrive for an employment interview?

**SELF-DISCOVERY EXERCISE No. 1:**

**HOW WELL DO YOU RECOGNISE YOURSELF?**

(Allow yourself not more than 15 minutes)

Imagine you're about to meet a company executive for the first time in connection with a prospective job. Please try to describe your physical appearance in a few sentences (100 words maximum) so that the person you're due to meet will be able to recognize you easily from your own physical description of yourself.

How did you find that? Not too difficult? How much more difficult to describe ourselves not in physical terms, but intellectually, emotionally and spiritually. Yet we're bound to confront these vital dimensions if we're to make even moderately sensible decisions about our future working lives. We should therefore proceed with a major stock-taking of our lives by asking how well we know our personal strengths and weaknesses. Here are some questions taken from a current selection procedure. Let's see how you cope—without a time limit!

**SELF-DISCOVERY EXERCISE No. 2:**

**HOW WELL DO YOU KNOW YOURSELF?**

(A) YOUR OWN ABILITIES AND LIFE INTERESTS

1. What kind of tasks or activities do you know subjectively that you enjoy doing?

2. Which of these tasks do you enjoy most? (Place the first three in rank order—i.e. first, second and third.)
3. What kind of tasks or activities do you know objectively, from independent evidence, that you're good at doing?
4. Which of these tasks are you best at? (Place the first three in rank order—i.e. first, second, third.)

(B) YOUR OWN ACHIEVEMENTS, SETBACKS AND LIFE VALUES

5. What have been the most significant achievements and setbacks in your life so far?
6. Which of these setbacks and/or achievements are most significant? (Place the first three in rank order—i.e. first, second and third.)
7. Which of your most cherished personal values guide you in your working life?
8. Which of these values are the most significant? (Place in rank order—i.e. first, second and third.)
9. Why do these values matter so much to you?
10. Are you able to identify the primary sources from which these most cherished values spring?

(C) YOUR OWN PREFERRED AREAS OF PAID EMPLOYMENT

11. Can you clearly identify those sectors and kinds of work which you would prefer to do (or not do)?
12. Which of these kinds of work attracts you most? (Place the first three in rank order—i.e. first, second and third.)
13. Are you able to explain why these kinds of work attract you most?
14. Assuming there were no professional, geographical or personal restrictions, what type of work would you most like to do?

## WHAT'S YOUR DOMINANT PERSONALITY TYPE?

Another route to a better understanding of ourselves is via the concept of dominant personality types. How would you describe your own personality type? If you don't know, how do you go about finding out?

For over 2000 years—from the speculative theories of the ancient Greeks to advanced contemporary research in applied psychology—

we can trace a sustained effort to understand human behaviour by means of the observation and classification of certain well-differentiated personality types. Most of us, of course, are a mixture or composite of several 'idealized' personality types. We show different facets of our complex personalities according to our mood—or the quarters of the moon. To help us with our analytical categories, however, it is useful to think of human beings in terms of 'dominant personality types' based on the observation of certain persistent patterns of behaviour.

The ancient world (and modern astrologers) believed that we are all born under the benign or baneful influence of certain celestial bodies—sun, moon and stars—whose conjuncture at our birth both explains and determines all our subsequent behaviour and our eventual fate.

The medieval world evolved an elaborate classification of human personality types, based on the observation of four clearly-differentiated 'complexions' or temperaments:

- *Choleric*—or hot-blooded types—tended to be quick to anger and were therefore well-suited to fighting or a military career.

- *Sanguinary*—or cool-blooded types—were ruddy of countenance and of a courageous, hopeful or amorous disposition and therefore well-suited to civilian employment.

- *Splenetic* types tended to be of a morose or peevish disposition—tending towards testy, irascible behaviour.

- *Melancholic* types tended towards sad, gloomy or depressed personality and were never good company at social occasions.

Not until the 19th century did more scientific theories of genetic inheritance emerge which encouraged psychologists to offer explanations of human behaviour based on the complex interaction of 'nature' (i.e. our inherited characteristics) and 'nurture' (i.e. our learned characteristics). By the end of the century, educational psychologists had pioneered the use of intelligence tests, based on the observation of how well the candidate performed certain intellectual tasks compared with his/her peer group.

In two World Wars (1914–1918 and 1939–1945), occupational psychologists advised governments on the selection of officers for the armed forces, based on psychological testing or personality typing. In the post-war decades, governments carried over the use of psychological testing from war to peace. Despite much controversy surrounding such tests—largely based on their questionable reliability as predictors of future performance—they were eagerly taken up and developed by industrial psychologists for use in the selection of potential managers and supervisors, including graduate trainees for the Civil Service, nationalized industries and large corporations.

Over the past 20 years, there has been a considerable upsurge of interest in personality typing, especially in the United States. Much of this new interest is stimulated by the need to identify and develop more young people with leadership potential—for example, to fill key vacancies in the space programme, the armed forces and business. This modern work is indirectly based on the pioneering work of the distinguished Swiss philosopher–psychologist Karl Gustav Jung. He was especially interested in exploring the dual nature of human personality—the bright side versus the dark side—the YIN/YAN—the balance of masculinity/femininity in the make-up of all adult humans.

Jung developed the concept of the 'wholeness' or balance of human bi-polar personality types. Most of us, for example, are a mixture of *introversion* (a tendency to turn inwards and direct our energies primarily towards the inner world of reflection, thought and feeling) and *extroversion* (a tendency to turn outwards and direct our energies primarily towards the outer world of people, things and activities). Which of these bi-polar opposites comes closest to *your* dominant personality type? To help you answer that question, we propose to explore two career-choice models which are already well-known in the United States but still much less well-known here in Britain.

## THE HOLLAND MODEL

An American psychologist, John Holland, has developed a useful theory of occupational choice, from which THE PARTY is derived, based on four assumptions:

- That most people can be described in terms of relative similarity to one or more of six idealized occupational-interest personality types.

- That there are six occupational environments.

- That people search for environments that will allow them to exercise their skills and abilities, express their attitudes and values, and take on agreeable problems and roles.

- That a person's behaviour is determined by an interaction between the individual's personality and the environmental characteristics.

# SELF-DISCOVERY EXERCISE NO. 3:

## THE PARTY

Below is an aerial view (from the floor above) of a room in which a party is taking place. At this party, people with the same or similar interests have (for some reason) all gathered in the corner of the room as described below.

R — People who have athletic or mechanical ability, prefer to work with objects, machines, tools, plants, or animals, or to be outdoors.

I — People who like to observe, learn, investigate, analyze, evaluate, or solve problems.

C — People who like to work with data, have clerical or numerical ability, carrying things out in detail or following through on others instructions.

A — People who have artistic, innovating or intuitional abilities, and like to work in unstructured situations, using their imagination or creativity.

E — People who like to work with people—influencing persuading or performing or leading or managing for organizational goals or for economic gain.

S — People who like to work with people--to inform, enlighten, help, train, develop, or cure them, or are skilled with words.

1. Which corner of the room would you instinctively be drawn to, as the group you would most ENJOY being with for the longest time? (Leave aside any question of shyness, or whether you would have to talk with them.) Write the LETTER for that corner in this box:

2. After 15 minutes, everyone in the corner you have chosen, leaves for another party cross town, except you. Of the groups THAT STILL REMAIN now, which corner or group would you be drawn to the most, as the people you would most enjoy being with for the longest time? Write the LETTER for that corner in this box:

3. After 15 minutes, this group too leaves for another party, except you. Of the corners and groups which remain now, which one would you most enjoy being with for the longest time? Write the LETTER for that corner in this box

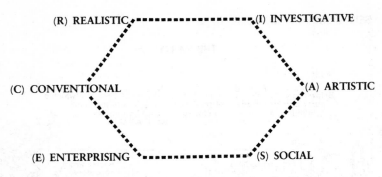

*Figure 5.1.* Holland's Six Occupational-Interest Personality Types

## Here are Holland's attributes of the six personality types:

### REALISTIC TYPES
— enjoy creating things with their hands;
— would rather work with objects (tools or large machines) than with ideas or people;
— like to work outdoors;
— tend to be rugged, practical, physically strong.

— *perceive themselves to be:*
  practical; frank; conforming; persistent; stable; responsible; concrete; aggressive; physically active; conventional in attitudes.

— *prefer occupations like:*
  Fish and Wildlife Manager; Laboratory Technician; Engineering Specialists; Armed Forces; Agriculture; Skilled Trades.

### INVESTIGATIVE TYPES
— would rather work alone than with others;
— have questioning minds;
— like loosely-defined problems which they can solve by working with ideas, words and symbols;
— do not like 'rule-following' situations;
— are frequently original and creative, especially in scientific areas.

— *perceive themselves to be:*
  rational; systematic; reserved; imaginative; intellectual; active; liberal in attitudes; alert; analytical; precise; cautious; independent; introspective; methodical; task oriented.

— *prefer occupations like:*
Biologist; Mathematician; Psychologist; Research Laboratory Worker; Physicist; Physician; Design Engineer; Technical Writer; Metereologist.

## ARTISTIC TYPES
— are artistically inclined;
— like to work alone in settings conducive to creativity;
— do not like situations requiring the use of physical strength.

— *perceive themselves to be:*
imaginative; original; introspective; independent; complicated; expressive through media; liberal in attitudes; non-conforming; idealistic; disorderly; self-sufficient; avoiding structure.

— *prefer occupations like:*
Artist; Author; Cartoonist; Composer; Singer; Poet; Actor; Actress; Orchestral Conductor.

## SOCIAL TYPES
— are usually able to express themselves well with words;
— get along well with others;
— enjoy being the centre of attention in a group;
— prefer solving problems through discussion or by arranging or rearranging relationships between others;
— have little interest in situations requiring physical activity or working with machinery.

— *perceive themselves to be:*
friendly; helpful; trustworthy; capable; persuasive; idealistic; seeking attention; expressive of feelings; caring; kind; insightful; sociable; understanding; leader; skilful speaker.

— *prefer occupations like:*
School Superintendent; Clinical Psychologist; Secondary Teacher; Marriage Counsellor; Playground Director; Speech Therapist; Vocational Counsellor.

## ENTERPRISING TYPES
— are good at leading and convincing people;
— are enthusiastic, self-confident, and dominant;
— think up new ways of doing things;
— are full of energy and like adventure;
— are impatient with work involving many details, long periods of intellectual effort, long periods of concentration.
— prefer social settings where they can lead and direct others;
▶ — like power, status, material wealth, working in expensive settings.

*— perceive themselves to be:*
energetic; domineering; sociable; aggressive; persuasive; materialistic; challenge-seeking; self-confident; verbally skilful in leading others; talkative; argumentative; adventurous; impulsive; progressive; risk-taking; pleasure-seeking.

*— prefer occupations like:*
Business Executive; Merchandise Buyer; Hotel Manager; Industrial Relations Consultant; Political Campaigner; Estate Agent; Sports Promoter; Television Producer; many kinds of Sales work; Law.

## CONVENTIONAL TYPES
— like jobs where they know exactly what is expected of them;
— prefer problems involving/requiring the use of verbal and numerical skills rather than those involving physical skills;
— have little interest in intense relationships with others;
— value material possessions and status;

*— perceive themselves to be:*
persistent; preferring low motivation for achievement; preferring structure; neat; conscientious; non-flexible; under supervisory pressure to achieve; influenced by others; shy; practical; self-controlled; conforming; effective in well-structured activities.

*— prefer occupations like:*
Bank Examiner; Bank Teller; Book Keeper; Financial Analyst; Computer Operator; Inventory Controller; Tax Expert; Statistician; Traffic Manager; some Accounting jobs.

## MYERS–BRIGGS TYPE INDICATOR
Two Californian psychologists, Katherine C. Briggs and her daughter, Isabel Briggs Myers, have gone back to Jungian dominant personality typology to develop an elaborate personality type indicator, with important vocational implications, based on the permutation of four bi-polar dimensions of dominant personality type:

| (E) | Extroversion – Introversion | (I) |
|-----|------------------------------|-----|
| (S) | Sensing – Intuition | (N)* |
| (T) | Thinking – Feeling | (F) |
| (J) | Judging – Perceiving | (P) |

*(N) for Intuition because (I) has already been used for Introversion.*

The Myers–Briggs Type Indicator (MBTI) has been widely adopted throughout North America and is gaining rapid acceptance amongst

Directors of Human Resources in western European countries and around the world. There are thus three important reasons why job hunters should make themselves thoroughly familiar with MBTI:

- *First*, as part of your overall effort to increase your self-knowledge, MBTI will help you gain considerable insight into your own dominant personality type.

- *Second*, becoming better acquainted with your own dominant personality type via MBTI should increase your self-confidence and allow you to discuss your strengths and limitations at interview with much less embarrassment.

- *Third*, you should have no difficulty in coping with a potential employer who invites you to complete the MBTI procedure.

## MBTI: WHAT IT IS—AND ISN'T

You must understand that MBTI is not a 'test' but a self-assessment inventory. You're not being judged. There's no normative scale against which you're being measured. The outcomes are not computed mathematically against some ideal score, indicating relative success or failure. MBTI simply yields useful information, to be put alongside other evidence, to help you understand and come to terms with your dominant personality type. And hence make a better-informed career choice. In the words of Katherine C. Briggs and Isabel Briggs Myers:

> There are no 'right' or 'wrong' answers to the questions in this inventory. Your answers will help show you how you like to look at things and how you like to go about deciding things. Knowing your own preferences and learning about other people's can help you understand where your special strengths are, what kinds of work you might enjoy and be successful doing, and how people with different preferences can relate to each other and be valuable to society.[1]

MBTI does *not* claim to predict the ideal career for you. Nor will it secure you that special job you've got your eye on. But it should refresh and reveal parts of yourself that other forms of assessment never reach. What's more, it indicates the broad field of work in which you're more likely to find satisfaction and scope for your abilities.

[1]Adapted and reproduced by special permission of the Publisher, Consulting Psychologists Press, Inc., Palo Alto CA 94306, from *Myers–Briggs Type Indicator*. Abbreviated Versions by Katherine C. Briggs and Isabel Briggs Myers (©1983).

In the hands of a skilled analyst and sympathetic career counsellor, the results of the MBTI represent useful information about you which may then be used to help form the basis for a much better-informed career choice. You may find that your predominant type is ST (i.e. a combination of Sensing + Thinking); or an SF (i.e. a combination of Sensing + Feeling); or an NF (i.e. a combination of Intuition + Feeling); or an NT (i.e. a combination of Intuition + Thinking). Figure 5.2, for example, suggests some vocational implications of personality type preferences, as revealed by MBTI.

| | If your personality type is: | | | |
| --- | --- | --- | --- | --- |
| | ST | SF | NT | NT |
| You're amongst people who prefer: | SENSING + THINKING | SENSING + FEELING | INTUITION + FEELING | INTUITION + THINKING |
| focus their attention on: | Facts | Facts | Possibilities | Possibilities |
| and handle these with: | Impersonal analysis | Personal warmth | Personal warmth | Impersonal analysis |
| Thus they tend to become: | Practical and matter-of-fact | Sympathetic and friendly | Enthusiastic and insightful | Logical and ingenious |
| and find scope for their abilities in: | Technical skills and objects | Practical help and services to people | Understanding and communicating with people | Theoretical and technical developments |
| for example: | Applied science/ Business/ Production/ Construction | Patient care/ Community care/Sales/ Teaching | Behavioural science/ Research/ Literature and art/Teaching | Physical science/ Research/ Management/ Forecasts and analysis |

*Figure 5.2.* **Some vocational implications of Personality Type preferences**

## FURTHER APPLICATIONS OF MBTI

A number of academics, interested in giving visibility to MBTI, have taken the essential content of MBTI and developed it in a number of helpful ways. Professor Tom Carskadon, a Research Psychologist at Mississippi State University, has prepared a summary of some selected characteristics of persons of different psychological types, based on the four dimensions of the MBTI.

## SELECTED CHARACTERISTICS OF DIFFERENT PSYCHOLOGICAL TYPES

### EXTROVERTS
Direct their energy and attention primarily toward the *outside world* of people, things and activities.
Are people of *action*.
Are often gregarious, talkative, think best 'with the volume on'.
Are energized by people and activity, relax through them.
Prefer to act first, think about it afterwards.

### INTROVERTS
Direct their energy and attention primarily towards the inner world of reflection, thought, and feeling.
Work well with thoughts and ideas.
Think 'with the volume off', sometimes give you their opinions only if you ask them.
May find it difficult to remember names and faces.
May be exhausted by too many people and activities, relax and are energized through quiet, privacy, intimacy.

### SENSING TYPES
Perceive the world primarily through the five *senses*.
Are interested in *facts*.
Are realistic, practical, down-to-earth.
Are usually accurate, steady, precise, patient and effective with routine and details.
Like to keep things simple, dislike unnecessary complication.
Like to practice skills they already know.
Are often relatively traditional, conventional.
Are oriented toward the present, the concrete, the here-and-now.

### INTUITIVE TYPES
Perceive the world primarily through *intuition*.
Are interested in *possibilities*.
Are interested in abstract concepts, implications, relationships between things or ideas.
Are often creative and innovative.
Dislike routine, attending to detail.

Often work in bursts of energy and enthusiasm, need to feel inspired.
May exaggerate, recall things inaccurately.
Are oriented towards the future.

## THINKING TYPES
Take decisions and come to conclusions on the basis of *thinking*.
Are usually logical, rational, analytical, critical.
Decide things relatively impersonally, are less swayed by feelings and emotions.
May have difficulty recognizing and acknowledging people's feelings.
Can deal with interpersonal disharmony, can be firm and assertive when appropriate.
Need and value *fairness*.

## FEELING TYPES
Make decisions and come to conclusions on the basis of *feeling*.
Use personal values, personal likes and dislikes as the basis for decisions.
Make relatively less use of logical analysis in making decisions.
Are often warm, empathic, sympathetic.
Value harmony, are distressed by serious argument, interpersonal friction, may have difficulty being firm and assertive.
Need and value *kindness*.

## JUDGING TYPES
Approach the outside world with a *judging* attitude, trying to order and control it.
Make up their minds and come to decisions quickly.
May jump to conclusions, even be somewhat closed minded.
Plan ahead, make and follow plans.
Like to work steadily until finished, get things done as soon as possible, dislike working on many things at once.
Are usually well organized, dislike having things disorganized and unpredictable.

## PERCEIVING TYPES
Approach the outside world in a *perceiving* attitude, gathering information, trying to adapt to it.
Like to delay decisions, get more information, keep options open.
Are flexible, spontaneous, often good in emergencies or when plans are disrupted.
Work at many things at once, may start more than they finish.
May be prone to procrastination and/or disorganization.
Are often very adaptable and open minded.

*Source: Professor Tom Carskadon, Department of Psychology, Mississippi State University.*

## HOW CAN WE USE THIS SELF-KNOWLEDGE?

By now, you should have clarified your ideas about your own personality, acquired a keener perception of your strengths and limitations, and gained a more profound insight into your own dominant personality type. What follows? How does that knowledge, those insights, help you in practical terms with your own career choice and job search?

Now comes the tricky part! Of course, nothing's for certain in this life. But let's make a few reasonable assumptions. Let's assume:

1. That you're of average intelligence or above.
2. That you're reasonably healthy, of good appearance, without severe physical handicap or psychological disability.
3. That you've recently completed a course of tertiary education (whatever the subject, whatever the results).
4. That you've learned how to learn, are well-motivated and willing to work reasonably hard without selling your immortal soul to the corporation.
5. That you're genuinely seeking paid employment.

Then—other things being equal, fingers crossed, with a shake of the lucky rabbit's tail—the chances are you're going to land an intrinsically satisfying, secure and well-paid job with prospects. In fact, there are now *only two things holding you back* from achieving your career ambitions:

- Your *lack of self-confidence*—because you simply haven't enough experience of job hunting.

- Your *lack of a strategic plan*—because until now you've probably not realized that you need such a plan and are in any case used to thinking tactically rather than strategically.

We tackle each of these deficiencies, in Chapters 6 and 8, respectively, offering practical advice and assistance which will help you overcome these twin obstacles which currently prevent you from launching yourself into a successful career.

### SUGGESTIONS FOR FURTHER READING
John L Holland: *Making Vocational Choices*, Englewood Cliffs. NJ: Prentice-Hall. (1985).

K. C. Briggs and I. B. Myers: *Myers-Briggs Type Indicator*, Palo Alto CA: Consulting Psychologists Press Inc. (1983).

# Positive thinking and self-confidence

*You've got to ac-cen-tuate the positive!*
*E-lim-inate the negative!*
*Latch on to the affirmative,*
*Don't mix with Mister In-Between!*

Tin Pan Alley

Chapter 6 tries to do three things:

1. To distinguish fantasy from reality in occupational choice.
2. To explore the psychology of job search.
3. To show how positive attitudes produce success in career choice and job search.

We all weave our lives from a mixture of dreams and desires, fact and fantasy, hopes and aspirations and down-to-earth realities. And nowhere in our lives is this process of adjusting dreams to reality more apparent than in our career choice and job search.

The American occupational psychologist Ginzberg and his fellow researchers have provided one of the best accounts of what goes on inside the head of a typical college graduate who is faced with those critical career choice decisions:

> occupational choice is a developmental process, not a single decision but a series of decisions made over years, with each step in the process having a meaningful relation to those which preceded it and follow it... Through the years of his development, the person has been trying to learn enough about his interests, capacities and values and about the opportunities and limitations in the real (external) world to make an occupational choice that will yield him maximum satisfaction... The process of occupational decision making could be analyzed in terms of three periods or phases—those of fantasy, tentative and realistic choice.[1]

According to Ford and Box:

> occupational choice may be seen as the culmination of a process in which hopes and desires come to terms with the realities of the occupational market situation... In other words, occupational choice is not random.[2]

In attempting to reconcile fantasy and reality, every job hunter must first recognize *the critical importance of 'self-imaging'*—a process which goes through three distinct phases:

- In *Phase 1* we explore *the concept of the self* as it develops and changes in a continuously evolving environment.

- In *Phase 2* comes *'self-differentiation'*—the realization that *one is a separate entity from other persons*, and then learning the specific ways in which one resembles and is different from others.

- In *Phase 3* we implement or actualize the self, *translating self concepts into occupational terms* as we move into the world of work.

---

[1]Cited by Cyril Sofer in his *Introduction* to W. M. Williams: *Occupational Choice*, London: George Allen & Unwin, (1973), p. 23.
[2]*Ibid.*, p. 35.

When we fail to develop a correct self-image—i.e. fail to come to terms with the true 'self'—we risk running into severe problems with career choice and job search. All too often, we set off down the wrong career track, pursuing a job in an occupation in which we're clearly not going to be happy or succeed—because it's simply not right for us. Even if we *do* succeed in finding a job in that occupation, we seldom achieve job satisfaction and may sometimes fail to understand why until it's almost too late.

When fantasy and reality come into head-on conflict in that way, we may easily fall victim to depression and failure because we're consuming so much time and energy trying to be what we're not. In other words, we've developed a very distorted 'self-image' which, by our very nature, we cannot possibly live up to. This, in turn, saps our energy, reduces our job performance and so increases our sense of failure. It takes considerable courage to admit defeat and to start over again by developing a more realistic 'self-image'. Many people, who never face up to this reality, lead lives of quiet desperation.

It makes good sense to avoid falling into that trap in the first place, if we possibly can. This means achieving a more realistic understanding of ourselves and making career decisions which are in line with a more positive 'self-image'. Let's look, for example, as that common situation which sometimes arises quite early in our careers, in which we wrongly assume we're not succeeding *simply because we're not really bright enough* to complete our course of studies. Consider the stories of Luke and of Millicent, each of whom encountered some difficulties in reconciling fantasy and reality.

## Luke's story

Luke was the younger son of a gifted family: both parents held top professional jobs—his father being a university professor and his mother a senior academic administrator. Luke's brother was clearly following in parental footsteps: he went from school directly into veterinary college and had little difficulty keeping up with the pace of academic work or passing his exams.

Luke was different. Despite his attractive personality, obvious charm and intelligence, he had considerable difficulties coping with school exams and certainly had no clear ideas about career choice. Because his school-leaving exam marks were low, he failed to qualify for university. Having no clear professional ambition, Luke had great difficulty deciding what course of higher education or vocational training to pursue. He finally settled for a course in Business Studies at a local college and got off to a fairly good start.

By the end of his second college term, Luke knew he was not cut out for the academic life. He lost interest in his chosen subjects, failed to attend lectures, and received formal written warning that he might be thrown out of college unless his work improved.

Not surprisingly, Luke failed all his first year exams. At a family counselling session, he eventually conceded that one reason for his failure was a persistent feeling of inadequacy—i.e. that he was less intellectually gifted than the rest of the family. He had only gone to college because he thought it was expected of him. What he really wanted was a practical job in the hotel and catering industry, where he could be trained and eventually work his way up into top management.

### Millicent's story

Born into a modest working class family, Millicent did well at school and was encouraged to enter Teacher Training College. She enjoyed the academic work but, since she couldn't see herself finding fulfilment in teaching, she moved across into librarianship.

Blessed with a sparkling personality, Millicent was extremely popular amongst her colleagues, one of whom—a man almost 10 years her senior—she married before she was 20 and before she had completed her librarianship qualifications. She was soon mothering two bonny daughters—only to find herself suddenly widowed at the age of 29.

Over the next few years, Millicent struggled to keep her family life together. Once, when taking her younger daughter to the local children's hospital, Millicent first came into contact with terminally sick children. She at once made up her mind to work at the hospital in a part-time clerical capacity.

Within five years of her husband's death, Millicent returned to full-time education to complete a BA degree. She worked extremely hard, coping with her studies, caring for her family and—since she received no financial grant whatsoever—working part-time for Marks & Spencer.

On completing her BA, Millicent tried working in the Financial Services sector but found selling pension plans and insurance schemes distasteful and unrewarding.

Finally, at the age of nearly 40, Millicent enrolled as a Student Nurse. When qualified, she believes she will achieve job satisfaction, having at last succeeded in reconciling fantasy and reality.

Courage was long ago defined as knowing what to fear and what not to fear. That's fine—but it doesn't help explain why some job hunters work themselves up into a fine frenzy when faced with the prospect of a job interview or allow themselves to degenerate into such a low mental state if they are rejected. One explanation might be that simply *because* we have so much at stake, our emotions sometimes impair or cripple our intellect. To minimize this risk, we need to understand more about the psychology of job search.

Psychological pressure and anxiety are both inevitable and invaluable parts of common human experience. When those pressures and anxieties exceed our capacity to handle them, we may become stressed and so reduce our effectiveness and efficiency as job hunters. The vicious circle is complete. You become desperate and—unless you're a consummate actor—your desperation shows. What can you—what should you—do in such circumstances?

To start with, let's admit our anxieties, let's face up to our fears. Fear of what? Of not finding the career path that suits us best; of not securing the preferred job in the organization of our choice; of not being selected at interview—in short, fear of failure, of being left behind, especially when our contemporaries appear to be so successful in fulfilling their own career aspirations and of landing the good jobs which seem to elude us.

And yet we know in our hearts that we have what it takes to succeed; we possess the innate ability; we've demonstrated our capacity to surmount obstacles and to overcome difficulties; we've prepared for—and passed—our final examinations. So why this irrational fear of failure? Perhaps, in the immortal words of President Franklin Roosevelt, we have nothing to fear but fear itself?

Speaking frankly about his own perennial stage-fright—the dry mouth and the butterflies-in-the-tummy whilst waiting in the wings to go on—the late Lord Olivier advised young actors and actresses to acknowledge their fears, to harness them, to make them work for us. What's true for acting is certainly true for real life. Why not turn your genuine interview anxieties to advantage and *make them work for you, not against you*? Why not transform your negative fears and anxieties into sources of positive energy? By inversion, they can become 'the wind beneath your wings'.

How to do it? Like most other useful life skills, technique doesn't come easily—but it certainly comes with practice. Acknowledge your doubts by all means. Express the negative emotions privately but aloud. Allow yourself the opportunity to hear your own voice admitting freely: 'Yes, I may fail in my objective today. But that doesn't mean I'm a failure.' But then match every doubt with its equal and opposite counterpart: the inversion or positive expression of that very same doubt. Make the positive thought the one that comes second and which stays with you longest: 'I'm going to do everything in my power to succeed today. *Yes, I am good enough for this job. Yes, I am qualified for this career. Yes, I do have a proven track record.* I can sustain my self-confidence by looking back on my achievements. And I *do* have the will to succeed in the future, just as I've succeeded in the past.'

## HOW POSITIVE ATTITUDES PRODUCE SUCCESS

That power of positive thinking is something you should practice at times which are less significant in your life. So that, when a truly critical moment arrives, like a final job interview, you've learned the drill and you know how to use it. Result? You positively radiate quiet self-confidence at your interview. And that positive attitude—the very product of your original fears—works for you. Interviewers cannot help noticing your self-possession in response to tricky questions. They cannot fail to be impressed by the way you control your breathing, your facial composure, your body-language. And you'd be surprised how much you give away about yourself by these means!

Occupational psychologists describe these body movements as 'displacement signals'—because they displace a surcharge of emotional energy or feelings. In other words, during an intensive period of questioning, you may say very little. But your body is doing a great deal of talking. You need to learn how to use your body-language—including that most precious asset, your smile—and to become fluent in its positive use.

A self-confident person, for example, does not maintain one fixed body position throughout a 20 minute interview. Watch your favourite TV news reader or political commentator. Note how he/she leans back in the chair, expressing self-confidence, and then comes forward, often with a positively emphatic hand-gesture, to illustrate or to underline a specific point. These 'illustrators' provide your interviewer with a good deal of useful information about your personality, your character, what's going on inside your head.

If you're going abroad for an interview, you need to be especially alert—because body-language is heavily culture-bound. Just as you shake hands and use more formal titles in continental European countries (e.g. in France, in Germany and, to a lesser extent, in Italy), so you must observe the niceties of body-language or risk being grossly misunderstood. Expression is still much more restained, formal and correct, in both verbal and body-language terms, than it is in Anglo-Saxon communities.

Conversely, in the United States (and, to a much lesser extent in Canada), you're likely to be addressed by your interviewer at a first meeting in familiar first name terms and you've then got to decide how to address your interviewer in response. (Normally, you'll be invited to call her/him Janet or John from the outset.) You must also learn how to blow your own trumpet more loudly and vulgarly in the US than you would do back home. Since the United States is a much more cosmopolitan, melting-pot society than the UK, you must expect to be asked much more directly explicit and personal questions and should be ready to use much less inhibited body-language at interview.

One final thought. According to Joseph Heller, the outrageously funny American author of *Catch 22* and other novels: 'Nothing fails like success.'[3] *We disagree. In our view, nothing succeeds like failure— provided, and it's a substantial proviso—provided we come to terms with that failure and learn to put the experience to good use.* Therefore, we urge you to acknowledge failure, to accept the judgement of others—but not to let such failure or such judgement oppress you or render you immobile. Use the self-knowledge which experience confers and the insight derived from limited failure to achieve unlimited success throughout your future career.

## SUGGESTIONS FOR FURTHER READING

Norman Vincent Peale: *The Power of Positive Thinking*, New York: World's Work (1952).

D. Bannister: 'Knowledge of self' in Cary L. Cooper (ed.): *Psychology and Management*. London: British Psychological Society and Macmillan. (1984).

[3]Joseph Heller: *God Knows*, London: Black Swan (1985) p. 105.

# Job hunters facing special problems

*It may be true that women face certain problems in jobhunting which their male colleagues avoid simply by being male, but it is also true that today's women jobhunters face a wider choice of jobs and life-styles than ever before. An exciting challenge indeed.*

Margaret Wallis: *Job Hunting for Women (1987)*

Chapter 7 tries to do three things:

1. To explain why certain job hunters face special problems.
2. To identify five groups who face such problems.
3. To suggest ways in which these groups can help themselves.

When it comes to choosing careers and searching for their first jobs, the vast majority of graduates face similar problems. They make the same kinds of mistakes, suffer the same sense of rejection, move slowly up very similar learning curves and eventually find themselves acceptable jobs in their chosen career fields. By definition, they constitute the majority of successful college leavers who find themselves good jobs within the first three to six months following graduation.

The majority of successful British job hunters are within the age-group 22–30; are unmarried and without children; are relatively free to pursue job applications, attend interviews and take up appointments throughout the UK or overseas if necessary. Life is certainly not trouble-free for the majority of graduates and every year, a small proportion of this majority fails to find themselves good jobs in the careers of their choice. They tend to hang around college after the start of the next academic session; are known to be depressed and suffer a common sense of failure; and keep one another company in certain well-known bars and cafés, sharing their tarnished dreams and disappointed expectations. Let's face it, some never find the jobs they're after and others take very much longer to launch themselves into successful careers.

The vast majority of graduates are nevertheless capable of solving their employment problems with a little help from their friends, from members of college staff and from career advisors. By the first Christmas following graduation, there may be as few as 10% who are still unemployed. This proportion will naturally vary from one part of Britain to another—with a smaller proportion of graduates still unemployed after Christmas in London and the south-east than in Liverpool and Manchester, Newcastle and Durham, Dundee and Edinburgh, Cardiff and Swansea.

Against this pattern of relative success, there are considerable numbers of graduates in other groupings who experience genuine and acute problems in their career choice and job search. We have identified five such groups whose special problems we deal with in turn.

## OLDER GRADUATES

Colleges throughout the UK are now accepting more and more students in higher age groups, via wider access schemes. Amongst these students will be found a certain number of single parents; a certain number who've been made redundant in mid-career; and a few students of the 'third age'—i.e. those who've already retired from full-time employment, are devoting some of their new-found leisure to studying, and who are not likely to be actively seeking jobs.

If you're more than ten years older than the majority of students on campus, you already know you're going to find it much more difficult to land your first job after graduation. The reasons are not far to seek. The vast majority of graduates find their way into organizations with graduate training schemes which cater for those aged 23–30. So, if you're aged 33–40, you're much less interesting to 'milk round' recruiters because you'll have fewer years employment in which to repay the cost of your training, although this attitude is now beginning to alter dramatically with demographic changes and the prospective shortage of sufficient younger graduates.

Perhaps that's self-evident and needs no elaboration. It nevertheless needs to be said that the majority of mature students are more strongly motivated than the average-age student. Furthermore, provided they've begun to overcome any psychological setback associated, for example, with earlier redundancy or bereavement, they have a number of things going for them which younger job hunters lack. Other things being equal:

- They have more life experience to draw upon and should therefore be able to prepare a more interesting *curriculum vitae*[1] than younger college leavers.

- They're likely to be more socially poised and therefore able to make a better self-presentation at interview than younger college graduates.

- They're likely to be more realistic about starting salary and conditions than some younger graduates.

In short, their very maturity may itself be a positive asset:

> They are emotionally stable, loyal, good at time management, show calm judgement and are good at getting on with other people. Who are these paragons of virtue? They are mature students. And these are the characteristics they commonly display as employees.[2]

According to a recent report by Barbara Graham of Strathclyde University, mature students are high-quality graduates. In 1987, graduates aged 30–34 had the highest percentage of first class honours

[1] *Curriculum vitae* or CV; see Chapter 12.
[2] Ngaio Crequer: 'Improved with age', *The Independent*, 14 September 1989.

degrees, and the 35–39-year-old group performed best in obtaining first and upper second class degrees. The report goes on to say that older graduates, especially women, are more likely to go into the public sector and are often found in the occupations providing personal services, such as education, health care and social services. Although there were some exceptions, a sample survey of a wide range of employers found that the private sector showed little interest in employing people over 30. Hence, these older college graduates find it takes them much longer on average to find the kind of job they're seeking or are willing to settle for. What can they do, what should they do, to help themselves?

- *First*, they need to start thinking about their future employment prospects much earlier in their college careers than their younger counterparts. They need to take stock, for example, of what they've done in their earlier pre-college lives, to help them decide whether to attempt to re-enter former employment—perhaps at a much higher level of responsibility—or whether to make a complete break into a new, unknown and untried career. The older the graduate, the longer this stocktaking is likely to take before they're ready to move on.

- *Second*, they need to develop a CV which tells the best possible story of their lives in as small a space as possible.

- *Third*, they need to turn their age and experience to good account by devising a more realistic strategy than their younger counterparts. Traditional college graduates have little or no experience of employment. Older graduates, by contrast, should plough their life experience into developing a more realistic, more flexible and successful career strategy.

- *Fourth*, they need to brush up on their interview skills and must not assume that their maturity and life skills alone will see them through. In most cases, older college leavers tend to be less inhibited when talking about themselves. In some circumstances, this may work against them: for example, they may talk themselves *into a job* in the first half of an interview and *out of a job* in the second half!

- *Fifth*, mature graduates should take advantage of their life experience to develop a strong network of contacts and to exploit these contacts in their job search, as described in Chapter 9.

- *Sixth*, remember that mature job applicants may be seen as posing a threat to some interviewers who may well be younger than them. They may also pose problems to some employers who perceive difficulties in successfully integrating an older recruit or trainee into a much younger workforce.

• *Seventh*, precisely because you are older, and may have experience of parenting and/or looking after elderly relatives, watch out particularly for jobs where your maturity is a positive advantage, e.g. in the field of education and training, in caring and social work, etc.


## WOMEN AS JOB HUNTERS

> Today
> It is maths and sciences
> Which are considered very important
> For those who want to get on in a technological world.
> Maths and sciences are the entry qualifications
> Which sort out those who are capable
> From those who are not
> > Dale Spender: *Gender and Marketable Skills: Who Underachieves at Maths and Science?*


According to the prestigious Henley Centre for Economic Research, women will make up half the British workforce by the end of this century. Since women now represent more than half of all traditional college students—and at least half of mature students—it might be assumed that they have no special employment problems to contend with. Don't believe it! Regrettably, sex discrimination continues to be found in almost every aspect of career choice and job search. The cruder forms of *direct discrimination*[3] may have faded amongst enlightened employers. But subtler and more elusive forms of discrimination have taken their place—for example, *indirect discrimination*.[4]

---

[3] *Direct discrimination* involves treating any job applicant, on the ground of his or her sex, less favourably than a person of the opposite sex would be treated in the same circumstances. Example: 'Male graduate required, with honours degree in chemistry, for teaching post beginning September.'

[4] *Indirect discrimination* arises where a requirement or condition of employment, applied equally to men and women, has in practice a disproportionately adverse effect on people of one sex as compared with the other, and cannot be shown to be justified in terms of the job to be done, irrespective of sex. Example: 'Ice-cream seller (part-time) wanted: must be 6 ft tall.'

Unfortunately, many women job hunters compound their own problems by the negative attitudes they display towards their own career choice and job search. For example, many women continue to talk down their domestic responsibilities, or the fact that they have managed to survive and succeed at college as well as bringing up a family, and keeping house, and all that implies in the way of conserving energy and managing limited time and a restricted budget, etc.

> If things are to change, women must change them, and if they haven't changed, a lot of responsibility must rest with women. If we take English, not science degrees, we won't benefit from teachers' incentive awards. If we don't follow university courses with a well-focussed training scheme, we won't be as well placed on the ladder as the men who do. If we don't know what we want, how will we get it?[5]

There are a number of discrete steps that women job hunters can and should take to enhance their employment prospects:

- *First*, don't reject out of hand certain kinds of employment simply because they've hitherto been traditionally male-dominated preserves. It's true that women are still pathetically under-represented in so-called 'top jobs' and other good jobs in this country. For independent evidence of this position, see *Appendix A*. The assumption should now be that—with the exception of a small number of jobs which are protected by 'genuine occupational qualification' status—all careers and all jobs are in principle now equally open to both men and women.[6]

- *Second*, don't fall into the opposite trap of assuming you'll be hired simply because you're a woman and a member of an oppressed minority. You won't. You'll be hired on your professional talent and your personal merits—or not at all. So, make up your mind to be as good as you can be at your job and compete on equal terms with both men and women. And may the best job applicant win!

---

[5] Jean Denton: 'It's up to women to change things', *The Observer*, 22 October 1989.
[6] Under Section 7 (1) of the Sex Discrimination Act 1975, an employer *may* lawfully discriminate in matters of employment where it can be shown that a person's sex is a genuine occupational qualification for the job—for example, in modelling clothes, or in dramatic performances or other entertainment for reason of authenticity—or where considerations of decency requires the job to be held by a man (or woman).

- *Third*, do join—if you can find one—a women's Self-Help Group in which women graduates compare their experience of job-hunting in a male-dominated world and learn from one another. If you can't find such a group, why not start one yourself? You'll be amazed how many others you'll find willing to join you. And it's further excellent administrative experience when it comes to writing your CV!

- *Fourth*, be prepared for sex discrimination and—if it occurs—be willing to stand up and combat it, not simply for your own sake, but for the sake of those who come after you. Every time a woman turns a blind eye or fails to act against sex discrimination, she implicitly condones it and makes life all the harder for those women who follow in her footsteps.

- *Fifth*, go and talk to a representative of the Equal Opportunities Commission and become better informed about the current legal framework surrounding women's employment. In particular, find out *how* how the Commission recommends you should deal with any evidence of discrimination in recruitment and selection policies and procedures—e.g. testing—before it happens, so that you know in advance how to act if and when the need should ever arise.

- *Sixth*, at interview, be prepared to use your femininity to your advantage—after all, men have not been fighting fair for years, have they? Make the most of your appearance. Remember, feminine wiles and feminine smiles may help you get a foot in the door. Dress smartly, use perfume discreetly—but no mini-skirts for over-thirties.

## BLACK AND ETHNIC JOB HUNTERS

If you're black or, indeed, a member of any other conspicuous ethnic minority, you'll need no reminder that you face a much more difficult employment future than most other college leavers. Let's not be mealy-mouthed: racism is still widely prevalent in British society—though many still prefer to call it 'colour prejudice'—as if that were somehow less offensive! What can you do to improve your chances of landing a good job in the career of your choice if you're black—and proud of it?

- *First*, don't assume that you'll encounter less racial discrimination, simply because you're a graduate. Other things being equal—which they rarely are where blacks are concerned—you should find a more liberal and tolerant attitude amongst educated colleagues—e.g. in the learned professions—than their less-educated counterparts. But be warned that racism, alas, knows no economic or social class barriers.

- *Second*, get to know your rights under current anti-racist legislation in employment matters and be prepared to deal with any incident involving racial discrimination—in advance of the event. It's not so easy to deal rationally and unemotionally with the correct complaints procedures once you're dealing with some specific incident in which you're personally involved.

- *Third*, take a positive attitude towards your career strategy and job search. To do anything else is to give up in advance. But be realistic about the length of time you may need to land the job you're really after.

- *Fourth*, try to stay in touch with your black contemporaries and be ready to exploit that network to help you slot into the career and the job of your choice. There's nothing unlawful about making use of anti-racist contacts to defeat and overcome racism.

- *Fifth*, take immediate steps to report evidence of racial discrimination to the Head Office of the Commission on Racial Equality (10–12 Allington Street, London SW1E 5EH, Tel: 01–828–7022) or to your local office.

## GAY AND LESBIAN JOB HUNTERS

Everything we've said about women and blacks applies equally to you—but with additional force! The discrimination you'll encounter is almost certainly more vicious and damaging than that encountered by other victims of discrimination. Because your needs are special and because the law concerning recruitment, selection and employment of those with your sexual preference is so obscure, we suggest you make early contact with your local Gay and Lesbian Switchboard (number in local telephone directory) and seek urgent advice on how best to deal with any discrimination you may encounter in employment.

## DISABLED JOB HUNTERS

Your problems are likely to be compounded by discrimination against those with any obvious form of disability plus the practical difficulties of physical access. You may or may not need to disclose details of your disability when submitting your initial job applications. However, depending on the nature of your disability, you may consider it wise to make a complete and frank disclosure right from the outset—and so reduce the risk of later disappointment. Once again, you need specialized advice and you should lose no time in establishing contact with the Disabled Graduate Data Bank

set up to provide disabled graduates and their career advisors with useful information about the kinds of work carried out by people with similar educational qualifications and functional handicaps.[7]

APPENDIX A: Proportion of women in some top jobs and other good jobs, 1983

| Occupation | | % |
|---|---|---|
| Bank Managers | | >1 |
| Members of Institute of Directors | | 2.9 |
| Members of British Institute of Management | | 2.3 |
| Institute of Chartered Accountants | | |
| (a) | Full members | 5 |
| (b) | Student members | 28 |
| Institute of Cost and Management Accountants | | |
| (a) | Full members | 2 |
| (b) | Student members | 15 |
| Institute of Civil Engineers | | |
| (a) | Full members | <1 |
| Institution of Electrical Engineers | | |
| (a) | Full members | <1 |
| (b) | Student members | c.3 |
| Institution of Mechanical Engineers | | |
| (a) | Full members | <1 |
| (b) | Student members | c.3 |
| Dentists | | |
| (a) | Practising | 8 |
| (b) | Students | c.35 |
| General Practitioners | | |
| (a) | Practising | 18 |
| (b) | Students | Entrants 45 |

[7] Chris Lillie and Elisabeth Standen: 'Data for Disabled Graduates', in *Graduate Opportunities*, Newpoint Publishing Company Limited (annually).

## APPENDIX A (*cont.*)

| Occupation | % |
|---|---|
| Surgeons | |
|   (a)  Practising | 1 |
|   (b)  Registrars | 35 |
| Barristers | |
|   (a)  Practising | 10 |
| Solicitors | |
|   (a)  With practise certificates | 12 |
|   (b)  Law students | 45 |
| Royal Institute of Chartered Surveyors | |
|   (a)  Full members | 1 |
|   (b)  Student members | 7 |
| Society of Surveying Technicians | ≪1 |
| Engineering Technicians | |
|   (a)  Practising | 2 |
|   (b)  Trainees | 4 |
| Architects | |
|   (a)  Practising | 7 |
|   (b)  Students | N/A |
| Veterinary Surgeons | |
|   (a)  Practising | 10 |
|   (b)  Students | c.35 |
| Advertizing Account Executives | 20 |
| Air Traffic Control Officers | |
|   (a)  Practising | 5 |
|   (b)  Trainees | 5 |
| Driving Examiners | 20 |
| Local Authority Chief Officers | ≪1 |
| University Professors | ≪1 |
| Civil Service | |
|   (a)  Executive Officers | 40 |
|   (b)  Under Secretaries | 5 |
|   (c)  Administrative Trainees | 40 |

N/A, not available.
*Source*: Ruth Miller and Anne Alston: *Equal Opportunities: A Careers Guide*, Harmondsworth: Penguin (1984).

## SUGGESTIONS FOR FURTHER READING

### Older Job Hunters
Older Graduates Working Party: *Bibliography*, Cambridge: Association of Graduate Careers Advisory Services (1985).

Older Graduates Working Party: *What Next?*, Cambridge Association of Graduate Careers Advisory Services (1986).

### Women
Margaret Willis: *Job Hunting for Women*, London: Kogan Page (1987).

B. Hopson and M. Scally: *Build Your Own Rainbow: A Workbook for Career and Life Management*, Leeds: Lifeskills Associates (1984).

Olga Aiken: 'Subjective Criteria in Selection: Cases in ethic and sexual monitoring', in *Personnel Management*, September 1988.

Margaret Korving: *Making A Fresh Start*, London: Kogan Page (1988).

Margaret M. Curran: *Stereotypes and Selection: Gender and Family in the Recruitment Process*, London: HMSO (Equal Opportunities Commission) (1985).

### Gay and Lesbian
Regrettably, no specific literature is known to the author and all suggestions are welcome. But your Gay and Lesbian Switchboard may be able to offer immediate help.

### Blacks and Ethnics
John Brennan and Philip McGeevor: *Employment of Graduates from Ethnic Communities*, London: Commission for Racial Equality (1987).

### Disabled
Mary Thompson: *Employment for Disabled People*, London: Kogan Page (1986).

For information on vacancies listed in The Disabled Graduates Data Bank, contact: The Careers Advisory Service, University of Nottingham, Cherry Tree Buildings (E), University Park, Nottingham NG7 2RD, Tel: 0602–506101.

# Career choice: Developing a career strategy

*Strategic thinking ... is nothing if not pragmatic. Strategy is a 'how to do it' study, a guide to accomplishing something and doing it efficiently. As in many other branches of politics, the question that matters in strategy is: Will the idea work?*

Bernard Brodie: *On Strategy*

Chapter 8 tries to do three things:

1. To clarify the distinction between finding a job and launching a worthwhile career.
2. To stress the vital importance of a career strategy.
3. To help you develop your own career strategy.

## FINDING A JOB *versus* LAUNCHING A CAREER

Anyone can find a job—and a 'good job', too! Thousands do so every day. Launching (or re-launching) yourself wisely and successfully into a worthwhile career—that's different—and much more difficult!

'Most men lead lives of quiet desperation,' wrote the idealistic young American, David Henry Thoreau. Today, he might simply add: '—and most women, too.' If Thoreau's statement is true—and a lifetime's observations appear to support it—how much of that despair is due to the wrong choice of career? We may never know for certain. But the present author's own research leads him to estimate that perhaps only ten in every 100 successful job applicants are quite sure they're in the right career.

The truth may be this: that, whilst some of us make an intelligent choice of what we sincerely believe to be the right career, in the light of all the evidence before us at the time, many of us have our careers chosen for us—or simply fall into some conveniently accessible career and make the best of it or live to regret it.

More accurately, we become increasingly aware, as the years go by, that there must be easier and more enjoyable ways of earning a living; that we *just might* have been more richly fulfilled in some other career than the one in which we still work.

That brings us to our first important point: when it comes to career choice, few of us devote sufficient time or care to the systematic, courageous and realistic evaluation of what's right for us. We'll devote up to 4 years of our lives preparing ourselves for the final examinations of an honours degree course. And we'll think that time well spent. But, let's be honest: apart from an occasional visit to a Careers Convention or that single desultory conversation with somebody at the University Careers Office, how many days do we devote to making a critically constructive and objective analysis of our deeper-felt needs and wants in paid employment?

How much time, you may ask, *should* one spend? That's a tough question to answer in quantitative terms. In qualitative terms, the answer is perfectly clear: as long as it takes to devise *an effective and successful career strategy* for yourself.

## SO, WHAT'S A CAREER STRATEGY?

Let's begin by distinguishing strategy from tactics. A strategy (or *strategem*) is a military term of art, meaning quite literally, 'the art of the general' (*strategia* (L) = the office or command of a general). *Strategy* is concerned with first-order priorities, in planning for peace or winning a war. The term may be accurately applied to the determination of high-level, far-reaching policy—the development of a master-plan—through the exercise of rational choice by those in overall command.

But a strategy cannot be devised in a political vacuum. It is not an end in itself but seeks to attain a predetermined set of aims or objectives, using a given set of resources, within a specific historical context. To accuse Napoleon of poor generalship because he failed to deploy certain artillery or cavalry against Wellington at Waterloo is to confuse strategy with tactics. But we may legitimately question his strategy when he invaded Russia with his Grand Army and penetrated as far as Moscow—only to be forced into that appalling 1812 retreat through the Russian winter. A hopeless General leading a hopeless army, defeated not by the Russians, but by a hopelessly flawed strategy.

*Tactics* are quite different from strategy. They are short-term, instrumental actions which help us achieve our strategic goals as soon as possible at minimum costs. They refer to a related set of instrumental actions, devised by those charged with implementing the predetermined strategy. They are thus second-order priorities, subordinate to the overall master-plan. They are essentially opportunistic, short-range, improvisatory moves, decided on the field of action in the heat of the moment. As defined by a recent Encylopedia of Modern War:

> Tactics refer to the conduct of fighting on or near the battlefield itself; strategy refers to the conduct of the war as a whole.[1]

If strategic planning involves the careful and detailed consideration of the entire range of options for achieving specific policy targets or objectives, what form is a *career strategy* likely to take in practice?

To start with, it is *never* short-term. It's *not* simply concerned with finding a job, however well-paid it might be. It *is* concerned with the fulfilment of certain carefully-considered, long-term, lifetime goals or objectives—such as securing employment in a designated field or specialist area of work and which:

1. Holds out the prospect of being reasonably secure.
2. Offers both immediately and in the longer term a set of worthwhile intellectual challenges and rewards, both material and non-material.

[1] Roger Parkinson: *Encyclopedia of Modern War*, London: Routledge Kegan Paul (1980).

3. Provides the means for achieving intrinsic as well as extrinsic job satisfaction.

4. Provides regular and sustained opportunities for the exercise of skills, the utilization of talents, the development of judgement, the chance to extend the range of your existing abilities—in short, to be stretched and to grow in the job without being subjected to excessive and avoidable stress.

5. Offers some reasonable prospect of progressive advancement to more senior, more demanding, better-paid or more rewarding work.

6. Brings you into contact with self-confident, self-critical but congenial colleagues who mostly share the same cultural norms and values, professional standards, and moral assumptions.

7. Allows adequate holiday entitlement, paid leave or sabbatical time off work to replenish your physical and mental resources, to maintain health and refresh the spirit.

8. Provides a secure stream of immediate and deferred income in the form of salary and pension payments, with adequate provision for life assurance, sickness and death benefit to offer peace of mind and security for your dependents.

Armed with this largely uncontroversial set of employment goals or objectives, how should we start to *think strategically, rather than tactically*, about our own career choice? Just as *military strategy* must be devised and shaped to keep the peace or win the war—and not just the battle—so *career strategy* must be devised and shaped to launch a career and not just to find a job. *Strategic thinking*, in other words, has to bridge the gap between where we now find ourselves and where we want to be at some defined point in the foreseeable future.

## STRATEGIC THINKING

This begins with a meticulous review and examination of three elements:

- *Our current physical, emotional, intellectual and spiritual resources.* Do we know ourselves well enough to be sure that we have what it takes to secure all or most of our employment objectives?

- *A realistic view of the current range of potential job opportunities.* Do we know enough about the possible range and diversity of the employment opportunities in which we might be able to achieve all or most of our employment objectives?

- *The relative importance of each of our employment objectives—the Musts and the Wants.* If we cannot realistically achieve all our employment objectives, what relative importance or weighting do we attach to each?

Only after working through these three elements can we begin to develop an effective and successful career strategy. That strategy can then be implemented by the choice of relevant and intelligent tactics in the form of job search—a subject to which we shall return in Chapter 9.

To develop our understanding of strategic thinking, let's work our way briefly but systematically through each of the three elements listed above.


## OUR CURRENT RESOURCES

If you've read Chapter 5, you'll know of the critical importance which we attach to self-knowledge and the need for a realistic understanding of your own strengths and limitations in the field of employment. On pages 76–77 there are some further questions, designed to test whether you can marshal the subjective evidence of the work tasks from which you derive satisfaction and the objective evidence of those work tasks in which you know you do well.

As you work your way through these questions, see whether you can discover more about your dominant personality type and then seek to make use of that information when you turn, later in this chapter, to devising your own career strategy:

---

**SELF DISCOVERY EXERCISE No. 4:**
SUBJECTIVE EVIDENCE OF TASK PERFORMANCE

Most people perform well at some work tasks, less well at others. You may not like doing a work task—yet still do well at it. But the chances are, you'll perform better those work tasks which you like doing. Indicate below how much you like doing each of the following work tasks.

THINK: Have I done this kind of task? Do I enjoy doing it? How much satisfaction do I really derive from doing it?

SCORE: 0 if not at all
       1 if not very much
       2 if average
       3 if fairly well
▷    4 if very much

|  | Doesn't apply to me | SCORE 0 1 2 3 4 | Don't know how to answer |
|---|---|---|---|
| 1. Asking questions | | | |
| 2. Investigating | | | |
| 3. Researching | | | |
| 4. Giving instruction | | | |
| 5. Explaining | | | |
| 6. Training | | | |
| 7. Offering advice | | | |
| 8. Counselling | | | |
| 9. Interviewing | | | |
| 10. Bargaining | | | |
| 11. Persuading | | | |
| 12. 'Selling' | | | |
| 13. Helping | | | |
| 14. Providing | | | |
| 15. Assisting | | | |
| 16. Directing | | | |
| 17. Supervising | | | |
| 18. Assessing | | | |
| 19. Co-ordinating others | | | |
| 20. Problem solving | | | |
| 21. Other (write in) | | | |

*Next, place the numbers 1, 2 and 3 against those work tasks which you would rank first, second and third. Finally, complete the following explanatory sentences: 'I get most satisfaction from these work tasks because* ...............................................................................................
..................................................................................................................................

## SELF DISCOVERY EXERCISE No. 5:
OBJECTIVE EVIDENCE OF TASK PERFORMANCE

You've indicated above how much you like doing certain work tasks. You now need to consider objectively how good you are at doing them.

THINK: How well did I really perform at this work task?
    Do I have independent evidence that I performed well?

SCORE: 0 if very poor indeed
    1 if not very good
    2 if average
    3 if fairly good
    4 if very good

| | Doesn't apply to me | | SCORE | | | | Don't know how to answer |
|---|---|---|---|---|---|---|---|
| | | 0 | 1 | 2 | 3 | 4 | |
| 1. Interpreting complex data | | | | | | | |
| 2. Making mental adjustments | | | | | | | |
| 3. Adjusting to new environment | | | | | | | |
| 4. Keeping secrets | | | | | | | |
| 5. Exploring new ideas | | | | | | | |
| 6. Summarizing complex ideas | | | | | | | |
| 7. Helping others understand | | | | | | | |
| 8. Coping with adversity | | | | | | | |
| 9. Clarifying an argument | | | | | | | |
| 10. Soliciting information | | | | | | | |
| 11. Offering guidance | | | | | | | |
| 12. Exercising judgement | | | | | | | |
| 13. Negotiating a contract | | | | | | | |
| 14. Making a public speech | | | | | | | |
| 15. Helping 'lame dogs' | | | | | | | |
| 16. Resisting sales pressure | | | | | | | |
| 17. Giving without reward | | | | | | | |
| 18. Self-sacrifice | | | | | | | |
| 19. Managing own time | | | | | | | |
| 20. Engendering co-operation | | | | | | | |
| 21. Giving orders | | | | | | | |
| 22. Keeping cool under pressure | | | | | | | |
| 23. Monitoring own performance | | | | | | | |
| 24. Admitting error | | | | | | | |
| 25. Disciplining subordinates | | | | | | | |
| 26. Other (write in) | | | | | | | |

*Next, place the numbers 1, 2 and 3 against the work tasks in which you think you perform first, second and third best. Finally, complete the following explanatory sentences: 'I perform best at these work tasks because* ...........................................................................................
....................................................................................................................................

## POTENTIAL JOB OPPORTUNITIES

Most, although not all, graduates will aim for the type of managerial/
professional work in which they can make use of three vital skills
which they should have mastered during their course of studies:

- The capacity to think critically and constructively and so to arrive at
imaginative solutions to complex problems.

- The capacity to work co-operatively with others in producing those solutions.

- The capacity to communicate those jointly discovered solutions effectively and cogently in speech and writing.

Even if you start your career at sub-managerial level, the chances are that you'll be identified as a potential candidate for promotion to supervisory/managerial rank. It therefore pays to take account of some of the similarities and differences between roughly comparable managerial positions in different sectors of the economy and in different organizations within those sectors. In the words of Dick Glover of CRAC:

> In essence you become a manager when you choose to do so—and you make that choice when you start to look for a job. You can go for jobs in companies where you can become a manager very quickly, you can decide to start your own business, or you can choose a career path in which you may not achieve managerial responsibilities for quite a long time.[2]

## RELATIVE IMPORTANCE OF YOUR EMPLOYMENT OBJECTIVES

Let's assume that you would ideally like to find a job paying not less than £12k p.a. within your chosen career field:

1. in the service sector rather than the manufacturing sector;
2. in the private sector rather than the public sector;
3. in south-east England rather than anywhere else in the UK;
4. in a rural rather than an urban environment;
5. in an area close to open water to allow you to water-ski;
6. in an area with low cost or subsidized housing.

Now consider this question: if an otherwise very attractive job vacancy should arise in the service sector (not in British Telecom, your preferred choice, but say, in the National Health Service; and not in the south-east but in Devon; and not in a rural environment but in urban Plymouth) would you automatically dismiss the possibility? Or have your weighted your MUSTS and WANTS and LIKES in such a way that will enable you to arrive at some kind of rational decision on whether or not to apply for such a job vacancy?

Here's how you might set about your weighting factors in the above example:

[2] Dick Glover, sometime Director of CRAC Insight Programme, writing on 'Careers in management' in the 1987 edition of the CRAC publication *GET* (*Graduate Employment and Training*).

- MUSTS *(weighting factor × 3)*
  1. Service rather than manufacturing sector.
  2. In the private rather than the public sector.
  3. £12k p.a. minimum salary.

- WANTS *(weighting factor × 2)*
  4. In south-east England rather than anywhere else.
  5. In a rural rather than an urban environment.

- LIKES *(weighting factor × 1)*
  6. Close to a river or waterway so that you can water-ski.
  7. With low-cost or subsidized housing.

## WHAT ABOUT SOME STRATEGIC PLANNING?

So, what range of strategic choice do we have to consider before arriving at an appropriate and relevant career strategy which will help us achieve our employment objectives? Your own strategic thinking somewhat obviously depends on a number of key variables:

- The general level of economic activity in the society—or part of the country in which you live or wish to live.

- The specific level of economic activity in the sector in which you wish to find employment.

- The supply of, and the demand for, well-qualified candidates in your chosen career field.

- Whether or not you have already worked in this career field before and have useful contacts on whom you may call for help and advice.

- How far you're prepared to compromise or settle for a job other than one in your chosen career field.

Many of us who feel comfortably secure in our chosen professions are periodically called upon to offer advice to those seeking a new career. Few of us, however, would risk the discomfort of seriously questioning whether *we ourselves* are in the right career. And some of us wait until we retire—or suffer the indignity of redundancy—before admitting that we may well have spent most of our lives in the wrong career! And, by then, it's too late to do much about it. How many genuine second chances does life afford? We should all aim to get it right first time, if we possibly can. As Dr James Welch, the educational philosopher, was fond of saying: *The product of the potter's wheel is not just the pot—but also the potter.*

## Robert's story

Robert was a fine man and a compassionate doctor doing an outstanding job as resident Medical Officer at the local mental hospital. Only child of a Sussex publican who had died on the Somme in 1917, Robert grew up in a household full of women—his mother, his grandmother, and his two maiden aunts. The experience may have proved useful in later life when dealing with his many women patients, who idolized him.

His family decided it would be nice if Robert became a doctor—an idea he never really questioned. At Cambridge he played cricket and read the English poets, especially Kipling, whose work he loved and knew by heart. He fell passionately in love with a fellow student; but she jilted him and he never got over it, remaining a bachelor all his life.

When I met him he was in his late forties, a stockily built, Saxon type of man with a mass of unruly hair. He lived alone in domestic chaos, surrounded by half-read books, medical journals, masses of germinating plants, unwashed plates, half-consumed meals, boxes of candied fruit and a large set of plastic buckets in which shirts were being steeped, prior to washing. He loved food and wine.

He told me he hated medicine and had always wanted to be a school teacher. He adored history and literature and his conversation was laced with academic allusions and literary anecdotes. He knew he had lost control of his life and career in his late teens. But the war had begun and doctors were in great demand. He was only half-reconciled to his life and was slowly eating himself to death. He died at the wheel of his car of a heart attack. He was just 50.

Let's take a somewhat frivolous example: suppose Mr Job Hunter and Miss Hope Springs, two Oxbridge Law graduates, *circa* 1990, decide—with characteristic Oxbridge arrogance—that they want to earn their living at the English Bar, make careers in politics, and enter Parliament with the aim of achieving Cabinet rank by the age of 40. To begin, they need to take very careful stock of the age structure of Britain's major political parties, before deciding which of them seems likely to offer the best chance of achieving their political ambitions by the year 2010. They might also look at their policies! But how well do they know themselves—and their chances of succeeding in realizing their ambitions?

Or let's take a less frivolous example. If you're mad about cars and are in your second year at a British University or Polytechnic, reading for a degree in Engineering or Business Studies, you might well decide that you want to move into the fast-reviving British motor industry after graduation. What strategic planning should you start to do, now? Here are six suggestions:

1. Visit the Business Library and read something fairly concise about the history, technology and current structure and problems of motor manufacture in Britain. There's masses of material; your friendly Library staff will help you locate it and no doubt come up with their own suggestions.

2. Go down to your College Careers Office and read the brochures on Graduate Recruitment at Ford, British Leyland, Nissan and Rover.

3. Make an appointment with the Careers Advisory Service and seek their advice on how to enrich your knowledge and understanding of the motor industry, how it works, and the kinds of qualifications, experience and attitudes you're likely to need for a successful career in that industry.

4. Find out wherever you can something about the life of middle managers in British manufacturing industry and ask yourself whether you think you'd be happy leading that kind of life.

5. Try to make sure you find some kind of vacation employment in one or other of the motor companies or one of their major suppliers—and find out at first hand, if possible, what life is like on the bottom rungs of the ladder in the motor industry—because that's where you'll inevitably start.

6. If you can't find a job with one of the motor manufacturing plants, try one of the major dealer networks. They can often use another pair of hands during peak summer selling months. Offer to carry out some sophisticated analysis for which their own staff simply don't have time.

## THREE MAJOR STRATEGIC OPTIONS

When it comes down to it, the effective range of strategic options available for achieving your career objectives is somewhat restricted. In effect, *we suggest there are really only three broad strategic options open to you.* We offer them here under familiar enough names, each with its associated tactical choices:

## FIRST STRIKE STRATEGY

You decide, after careful consideration, that *you are uniquely and ideally qualified for one particular type of job(s)* in the appropriate industry, sector, organization and/or geographical area of your choice— and *you go flat out for that job(s)*, seeking to make your first strike well ahead of other well-qualified candidates, using all your considerable data-gathering resources to identify each and every one of the particular job vacancies that arise. For relevant job search tactics, see Chapter 9.

## FLEXIBLE RESPONSE STRATEGY

You decide, after careful consideration, that *you are not uniquely qualified or ideally suited for any one particular type of job(s)*—but see yourself rather as being more flexible, adaptable and versatile. You therefore *test the job market by applying for a whole series of very different jobs*—in different industries, sectors, organizations and geographical areas (both at home and abroad) in order to discover whether you like the look, the sound and the feel of any organization to which you choose to apply and which subsequently invites you to interview. For relevant tactics, see Chapter 11 on decoding job ads and submitting job applications.

## WAIT-AND-SEE STRATEGY

You decide, after careful consideration, that *you lack any clear view of the type of job for which you might be even vaguely qualified or suitable* but that, equally, you have no appetite for a protracted series of speculative job applications. In this case, *you decide to adopt a strategy of wait-and-see*—exploring a limited range of possible job vacancies through the technique known as 'Networking'. For relevant tactics, see Chapter 9. Or you may seek further professional career counselling of the kind offered by *Career Choice and Job Search*. For relevant information, see Chapter 16.

### SUGGESTIONS FOR FURTHER READING

Stuart Timperley: *Personnel Planning and Occupational Choice*, London: George Allen & Unwin (1974).

D. Brown and L. Brooks (eds): *Career Choice and Development*, San Francisco: Jossey-Bass (1981).

# Job search: Devising and implementing tactics

*Travailler est donc un devoir indispensable à l'homme social.*
*Riche ou pauvre, puissant ou faible, tout citoyen oisif est un*
*fripon.*
*(Every citizen has an inescapable duty to work. Whether you*
*are rich or poor, weak or strong, if you are idle you will be*
*considered a rogue.)*

> Jean-Jacques Rousseau (1712–1778): *Emile*

Chapter 9 tries to do three things:
1. To explain the meaning of purposeful job search.
2. To compare traditional and innovative tactics.
3. To help you devise your own successful tactics.

## PURPOSEFUL JOB SEARCH

Let's begin with a few optimistic assumptions and suppose:

- That you've closely followed the advice on career strategy given in Chapter 8.

- That you've developed your career strategy and now feel reasonably confident that you've decided on the right career for you.

- That you've set down on paper the broad range of jobs within the field of employment on which you've got your sights trained.

- That you've accurately targetted the sector(s), region(s) and industries—even the names of organizations, perhaps—in which you're going to seek employment.

- That you've made up your mind what weighting you'll attach to each of your employment WANTS or LIKES (as opposed to your more heavily weighted MUSTS) if you can't find precisely what you want, where you want it, and have to compromise.

- That you've checked and double-checked your responses and are now reasonably confident that you've reached the right conclusions.

What follows now? Logically enough, your next step is *to devise and implement appropriate tactics for a purposeful job search*. In other words, you must now work out a method and start tracking down one or more employers who are equally convinced that the only way their business can survive and succeed is by advertising a job vacancy just like (or very similar to) the one you're looking for. Hence the need for a *purposeful job search*. Like developing a career strategy, job search isn't as easy or straightforward as you might suppose.

Of course, if you've NOT developed an appropriate career strategy, you're certainly not ready to begin your job search. If you do, you'll embark on a purposeless job search. As a wise man once said, if you don't know where you're going, almost any road will get you there!

In Chapter 1 we said something about labour markets and how they work in theory and practice. There's rarely a perfect match between buyers and sellers of labour—partly due to market fragmentation and geographical separation but also because of 'imperfect knowledge'. In other words, how can you, Mr Joe Punter, currently residing in Little Piddletrenthide, Dorset, who's desperately looking for a job as a *Slagger Maker's Bottom Knocker*, possibly know that Mr Bill Bloggs of Newton-le-Willows, Lancashire, is searching equally desperately, for a well-qualified, time-served, classically-trained, fully-experienced *Bottom Knocker*, just like Joe, to work alongside one of his best *Slagger Makers*, Herbert Hardcastle? (You surely remember old Bert?)

Being aware that there's now a critical national shortage of skilled men in this key area of the pottery trade, Joe Punter might well begin by scanning the weekly *Ceramic Gazette*. That's where Bill Bloggs is most likely to advertise his current vacancy for a half-decent *Bottom Knocker*. What goes for *Slagger Maker's Bottom Knockers* applies equally to most other skilled occupations—from *Computer Programmers* and *Electronic Engineers* to *Molecular Biophysicists* and *Protein Crystallographers*, from *Financial Analysts* and *Weather Forecasters* to *School Teachers* and *Seismic Technologists*, most of whom have their own trade journals and specialist magazines in which relevant jobs are regularly advertised. Any good public library will advise you of the relevant trade journal for your own career specialism.

By now, you should know better whether you intend to concentrate your job search exclusively on one closely-specified type of vacancy (e.g. *The Andy Warhol Chair in Experimental Condensed Matter Physics in the University of Oxford*) or whether you'll keep a more open mind and give reasonable consideration to any job vacancy within the relevant field of employment (e.g. *any senior academic appointment within the general area of pure or applied physics anywhere in the English-speaking world*).

Let's be brutally honest: if you were born and bred in Scotland, have strong family ties there, want to marry a Scots partner, start a family and bring your children up within a bagpipe's throw of the Bonnie Banks of Loch Lomond then, quite frankly, you're wasting your time and energy pursuing any kind of job vacancy in London or the south-east of England. *You just will not be happy—however much they pay you!*

## WHERE DOES TRADITIONAL JOB SEARCH BEGIN?

If you're *not* a narrow specialist, if you *are* willing to consider any related work for which you may be reasonably well-qualified, and if you're *not* so unequivocally tied to any one area of the country, you should begin your *traditional job search* by considering the much larger number of less specialized job vacancies, in such areas of General Management and Administration as those to be found within the broad range of manufacturing, commerce and service sectors, both private and public.

All the national quality newspapers—*The Times, The Financial Times, The Guardian, The Independent, The Daily Telegraph, The Observer* and *The Sunday Times*—advertise various types of job vacancy on specific days of the week. *The Guardian*, for example, currently advertises its job vacancies as follows:

**Monday:** Creative, Media, Marketing, Secretarial

**Tuesday:** Education

**Wednesday:** Public Appointments

**Thursday:** Science, Technology, Computing

**Friday:** Legal Appointments

**Saturday:** Jobs and Careers

In addition to the heavyweights, there are the important weeklies—like *The Economist, The New Statesman and Society,* and the *Investors' Chronicle*—which are well worth looking at. So, it pays to drop in regularly (twice a week, at least) on the Periodicals Section of your University (or Local) Library. If there are too many details in the ads for note-taking, you'll generally have easy access to a photocopier, or you can buy your own copy.

When scanning newspapers and journals for suitable job ads, don't dismiss out of hand what might otherwise seem like a really worthwhile job simply because it's not *precisely* what you're looking for. If, for example, you're looking for work as a *Design Consultant* or a *Marketing Analyst* with a major British retailer—say, *Marks & Spencer* or *Habitat*—don't overlook a vacancy for a very interesting and related post with one of the major wholesalers or manufacturers who supply Marks & Spencer—say, the *Coats Viyella Group*, now Britain's largest textile and knitwear firm, or *Corah's*, who manufacture the universal underwear and those sensible socks we now all seem to wear! Once you're established in the right general field, you'll normally find it much easier to move across from one part of the industry to another than to break into the industry at exactly the right place.

Keep a close eye, too, on the *Business Section* of the major national dailies. In addition to daily company news and comment, they periodically publish *Special Surveys* of particular industries under witty or facetious titles such as *Foaming at the Mouth: British Brewing*, or *The Counter Revolution: Banking in Bangladesh*, or *The Way the Waffle Crumbles: Baking in Belgium*.

As well as checking the media for suitable job vacancies, remember that your college *Careers Advisory Service* or *University Appointments Office* will normally post weekly lists of vacancies which have been directly notified to them. And your local *Job Centre* will normally have a special display board devoted to *Professional and Managerial Appointments*. Both well worth checking out.

If you follow this traditional job-search route, you'll soon gather a great deal of information. So, you'll need to devise some means of recording and keeping track of what's happening in each of your areas of interest. You don't need anything as exotic as Filofax. Try something simpler but equally effective—like an alphabetical notebook, cross-referenced between organizational names and employment sectors. Combine this with a clear set of diary entries of where and when and why you applied for specific job vacancies or 'cold canvassed'[1] certain organizations. It's very easy to confuse yourself unless you keep clear notes on everything you do.

As your job search gets into its stride, you'll gradually build up a mental map of your chosen field of employment. This should enable you to maintain a fairly accurate assessment of the level of demand for well-qualified staff in different industries in various parts of the country. Use this continuous assessment to make regular corrections to your job search tactics.

## INSTITUTING A MORE INNOVATIVE JOB SEARCH

Some three-quarters of all job hunters in most specialist fields report that they succeed in obtaining a suitable appointment and start work in a new job through the traditional form of job search, described above. What should you do, however, if traditional job search tactics don't pay off? When should you adopt more innovative tactics? As soon as possible—for in this fiercely competitive world, you must adopt whatever tactics—traditional, innovative or eclectic—that you think will help you implement your career strategy and so achieve your employment objectives as soon as possible.

### TRADITIONAL VERSUS INNOVATIVE TACTICS
Having reviewed various traditional tactics, let's match them up with some of the more innovative counterparts:

[1] For an explanation of 'cold canvassing', see later sections of this chapter.

| TASK | TRADITIONAL TACTICS | INNOVATIVE TACTICS |
|---|---|---|
| Identifying vacancies | Scan the national media | Scan the local, national and international media |
| Submitting job applications | Neat, clean, British-style CV and crisp letter of application | Try North–American-style Resumé and less conventional letter of application (see Chapter 12) |
| Preparing for initial interview | Review earlier interview experience | Undertake additional interview practice (see Chapter 13) |
| Preparing for second interview | Rely on instinct to see you through | Undertake rigorous review of initial interview (see Chapter 13) |
| Preparing for contract negotiation | Trust to luck to see you through | Research value of total employment package (see Chapter 14) |

## FIFTEEN KEY STEPS TO NETWORKING

The gentle art of Networking comprises the building and exploitation of an interconnected set of personal contacts for the purpose of seeking advice and helping you to secure desired employment in the field of your choice. The way to set about your Networking is as follows:

1. Sit down with a large sheet of paper and a pencil.
2. WRITE your name in a small circle somewhere in the middle of the sheet of paper.
3. Now assume that small circle is the hub of a great wheel—or the sun rising optimistically over the green hills of summer—and throw half a dozen or so well-spaced spokes of a wheel (or the rays of the sun) radiating from the central hub.
4. Next, think carefully about the names of half a dozen influential people with whom you (and/or your immediate family) have regular

social intercourse, contact or dealings. In theory, they can be as diverse as your doctor, the captain of your local soccer team, your father's bank manager or mother's best schoolfriend. But the better placed they are in their chosen professions or occupations, the better.

5. Print their full names at the end of each of the six or seven spokes of the wheel you've just made (see Figure 9.1).

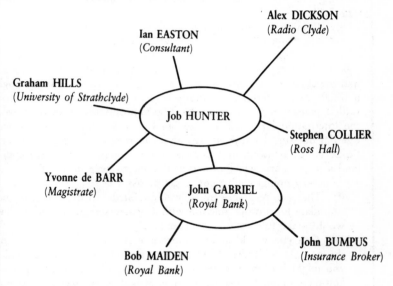

*Figure 9.1.* The gentle art of Networking

6. Now comes the creative part. Taking your time—and trying all the time to remember the likely effect of your letter on the unsuspecting recipient, as well as the sympathetic response you wish to evoke in the reader—draft a short personal letter in which you:

   (i)   Briefly (re)-introduce yourself.
   (ii)  Describe your current career dilemma.
  (iii)  Make it clear you're *not* asking for a job.
  (iv)  Say how much you would value some advice on some specific questions.
   (v)  Ask tactfully whether you may come along for a short meeting (say, 20 minutes) to seek personal advice on how best to proceed (see Draft Networking Letter below).

7. Once they know you're not importuning them for a job, which they know they'll have to refuse, most recipients of your letter will feel flattered to be asked for advice and agree to see you. Remember, they're busy people, so you really must make the most of your time.

8. The first person who agrees to see you is John Gabriel, your father's Bank Manager. Once you know the date and time of your meeting with Mr Gabriel, send him a copy of your CV for information. This will:

    (i) Remind him of your interview.

    (ii) Start him thinking seriously about you.

    (iii) Save time at the meeting.

9. At the very outset of the meeting, enquire politely whether he's had the chance to go through your CV and offer to take him through it briefly (a wonderful opportunity here to display your presentation skills!), pausing for relevant emphasis, as appropriate ('I greatly enjoyed the International Finance and got an Upper Second in that subject. But I'm not sure I know enough about merchant banking to be sure I'd be happy working in a finance house. Unless, of course, I could land a job in Paris which would enable me to keep up my French').

10. The key points you've got to get across are:

    (i) That you're a very lively, well-qualified and highly-motivated candidate for any suitable job with a progressive organization that would make full use of your talents.

    (ii) That you would greatly appreciate any advice in the form of the names and addresses of suitable persons to whom he thinks you might profitably write, sending a copy of your excellent CV, and mentioning Mr Gabriel's name, providing he gives permission.

    (iii) Meanwhile, if there are any personal introductions which might be arranged at once, you'd be particularly grateful to Mr Gabriel.

    (iv) You very much hope he will bear you in mind as he meets his other clients over the next few months or so.

    (v) Finally, you thank Mr Gabriel very courteously, saying you hope you may keep in touch with him to report how you've progressed with the contacts he may have suggested to you.

11. On returning home from the Gabriel meeting, you immediately update your Networking chart by adding the names of the people and the organizations recommended by Gabriel.

12. Next day, without fail, you write Mr Gabriel a short but sincere letter of thanks, repeating your request that he bear your name in mind for any contact or suitable job vacancy which may arise.

13. You then revise, sign and despatch an already drafted letter to the named contacts Gabriel has supplied, quoting Mr Gabriel's name, ► and asking whether you may arrange an early appointment to seek

advice about your CV (copy enclosed) and any help they may be able to offer.

14. At each stage of Networking, you repeat exactly the same procedure until, sooner or later—and usually sooner than you expect—somebody somewhere surfaces with just the right job for you.

15. There's nothing illegal or immoral about networking. It takes some effort—but it works. You're kept busy—and you help yourself by building a network of contacts that will prove invaluable—whatever job you finally settle for. And it works equally well for women as well as men. Possibly even better.

### DRAFT NETWORKING LETTER

22 Hope Spring Cottages<br>
The Dell<br>
Slaveringham<br>
Nottingham NG2 6HD

PERSONAL
Mr John Gabriel OBE
General Manager
The Royal Bank
Mercantile Chambers
The Pantiles
Nottingham NG1 2LR

9 June 1990

Dear Mr Gabriel:

You may recall that I came to see you with my father some four years ago, in connection with an educational trust which you kindly arranged on our behalf.

I'm happy to tell you that I graduated last month with a Lower Second Class Honours Degree in History and French at the University of Sussex and am now in the process of completing some important career decisions.

I'd like to make clear at the outset that I'm not looking for a job in banking. But I should nevertheless greatly appreciate it if you could kindly spare me some time next week for a brief informal chat in which I could have the benefit of your advice on a number of difficult options which now·face me.

I should therefore like to call on your Secretary next week to find out whether you will kindly spare me 20 minutes for an early meeting.

With all good wishes

Yours sincerely,

Job Hunter

So far we've talked about seeking help from family and friends, making use of college and commercial employment agencies, and experimenting with Networking. What if you've tried all these—and they're still not bringing in the kind of job offers you really want. What then?

One implication might be that what you have in mind is a certain style of job in a specific kind of organization—and they're simply not advertising that kind of vacancy right now. What can you do to break into the organization of your choice—BP or British Aerospace or Burroughs Wellcome or the BBC? The answer is Cold Canvassing—a technique perhaps better suited and more relevant to well-qualified candidates, with a good employment record, rather than those setting out to secure their first appointment following graduation. But you never know—and it's certainly worth a try!

This is how it works. You do your research and decide you have a very special set of competencies which might well be in demand by a limited number of organizations. They're the ones you want to work for—but they're just not advertising vacancies right now. What you have to do is to ring their bell in such a way that, even though they're not currently in the employment market, they may nevertheless be willing to see you and perhaps even hire you as a long-term investment.

Your CV, always immaculate, must now be edited to target precisely the organization you're addressing and the type of job you have in your sights. You then need an exceptionally attractive short letter which seizes the employer's attention without your seeming neurotic. In essence, you're writing to introduce yourself on paper and to ask for an informal meeting without commitment on either side, to discuss the possibility that you might be of some service to the organization, either immediately or at some date in the near future.

To demonstrate what's needed—and as an exercise in self-critical letter writing—what follows is the final draft of a 'Cold Canvass' letter, as prepared by a recent client candidate. Read this letter carefully from the viewpoint of the prospective addressee—and make some notes on its strengths and weaknesses. Then try your hand at re-drafting the letter in a way which reflects your own ideas of what such a Cold Canvass letter might say. We shall then offer our own critical comments on the candidate's draft and present our own suggested version. For maximum benefit, please don't read ahead in this chapter until you've completed the critical exercise for yourself.

## CANDIDATE'S FINAL DRAFT OF COLD CANVASS LETTER

22 Whitsuntide Court
Epiphany Road
Corstorphine
Edinburgh EH6 7KF

21 May 1990

Mr Jonathan Smith
Managing Director
Smith, Nephew and Aftermath
Management Consultants
40 The Square
London WC2 8LC

Dear Sir:

I am currently studying for the degree of Master of Business Administration and wish, on completion of this course, to make a career move into the field of management consultancy. I am keen to gain experience in this sphere by working with a large consulting firm and my purpose in writing is to enquire if you have a position in your organization for which you feel I may be a suitable candidate. I enclose a full curriculum vitae for your consideration.

During my five years as a company director, I gained experience in all aspects of business management, while developing strong interpersonal skills and an ability to motivate a team of people of varied ages and from diverse backgrounds.

In 1986, the decision was taken to update the practical experience gained to date with a formal business qualification, that of an MBA degree. The teaching part of the course will be completed in June of this year. This degree is very much biased towards the practical through the analysis of live case studies, rather than on theoretical rigour. Particular emphasis is placed on the development of both corporate and marketing strategic planning skills, while the core foundation class of accountancy has provided the necessary financial basis for the consideration of such cases.

I believe that my career pattern to date has demonstrated my ability to acquire and assimilate knowledge quickly. As a prospective MBA graduate with management experience, I feel I have both personal qualities and relevant business experience which could be fully utilized by your company. I would very much welcome the opportunity of an interview to discuss this further.

I look forward to hearing from you in due course.

Yours sincerely

Maureen Bedford

**CRITIQUE OF MAUREEN BEDFORD'S LETTER**

1. *As a cover letter it's too long. The message should be contained within one side of a sheet of notepaper, whether hand-written or word-processed.*
2. *The structure is weak and repetitious. It jumps back and forth between reporting and requesting.*
3. *The tone is wheedling. The message needs to be courteous but not obsequious.*
4. *There is too much content. It should highlight the CV but should not try to digest so much of it.*
5. *The letter is less than business-like for a management consultancy. It should be tightened up all round.*

**CAREER CONSULTANT'S SUGGESTED REVISION OF COLD CANVASS LETTER**

22 Whitsuntide Court
Epiphany Road
Corstorphine
Edinburgh EH6 7KF
21 May 1990

PERSONAL
Mr Jonathan Smith
Managing Director
Smith, Nephew and Aftermath
Management Consultants
40 The Square
London WC2 8LC

Dear Smith:

After seven years in publishing—the last five as Director of the Richard Dennison Publishing Company—I have decided to make a career move into management consultancy. My immediate aim is to join a major consultancy where I can diversify my experience and make the fullest use of my qualifications, skills and present experience. I enclose a copy of my CV for information.

At Richard Dennison, where my responsibilities covered all aspects of business management, I developed strong interpersonal skills and an ability to activate a team of people of varied ages and from diverse backgrounds. During my five years as Director, the company's business increased by 500%.

In 1985 I decided to requalify and strengthen my practical experience by studying for an MBA degree which will be complete in June. The degree is

94

strongly biased towards practical learning through case studies with particular emphasis on the development of skills in strategic planning and corporate marketing, with a solid foundation in accountancy.

I should very much welcome the opportunity of an interview to further explore this application and to seek your advice on how best to progress my career.

Yours sincerely

Maureen Bedford

Cold Canvassing is no panacea. It won't always open the doors you want. But it is, at least, a pro-active approach to job search. It gets you ahead of the brat-pack. And there's nothing to be lost except the cost of a few stamps and a few rejection letters. And, you never know: it may work! Indeed, some of our clients have reported back to us that Cold Canvassing seemed more like 'cold turkey' at the time; but that it paid off—and they're now happily ensconced in the organization of their choice. So, persevere and keep those well-composed letters flowing! Remember: always address them correctly to either the Chief Executive or Managing Director by name and mark them 'PERSONAL'. That way, even his Secretary may not open them! And he can always pass them down the line to the Director of Human Resources to reply on his behalf, if he so chooses.


## WHAT IF YOU'VE STILL NOT FOUND A JOB?

The answer must depend on your analysis of the outcomes of your traditional and innovative job search over the past several weeks or months—but hopefully not years. Different job hunters encounter different types of problem in different areas of employment at different points in the job market cycle. That's why you *must* keep those crucial notes referred to above! Without marshalling the symptomatic evidence, you can't make an accurate, intelligent and insightful diagnosis of what's going wrong—or prescribe an appropriate remedy.

Overleaf are a dozen of the most frequently-reported symptoms, the most likely diagnoses and some suggested remedies:

# WHAT TO DO WHEN YOU STILL CAN'T FIND THE RIGHT JOB

| REPORTED SYMPTOMS | LIKELY DIAGNOSIS | SUGGESTED REMEDY |
|---|---|---|
| 1. Can't identify suitable job vacancies | Not looking in correct places? Overlooking marginal job vacancies? | Review media with Careers Office and/or Librarian Be more venturesome |
| 2. Don't get round to sending for application form | Not keeping job log? Pursuing too many marginal jobs? | Institute job log |
| 3. Failure to submit application by closing date | Don't understand what's required until too late? Inexcusable laziness, procrastination or cock-up? | Seek professional career choice and job search counselling Get yourself better organized |
| 4. There *are* no suitable job vacancies at present | Employment sector is currently depressed? | Check out with Careers Office Review and adjust target vacancies |
| 5. Don't get invitation to initial interview | Not submitting an effective CV or job application? Inadequately qualified for vacancies? | Change content and/or style of CV and job applications Apply stricter criteria to job search |
| 6. Fail selection test/ procedures | Lacking in self-confidence? Panic? Lacking in experience of such tests | Seek professional career choice and job search counselling Seek professional career choice and job search counselling |
| 7. Don't get invited back for later interviews | Giving contraindications at interview? Failure to demonstrate enthusiasm | Review and adjust interview technique Need more and better interview experience |
| 8. Don't get job offers | Defective interview technique? | Seek professional career choice and job search counselling |

## WHAT TO DO WHEN YOU STILL CAN'T FIND THE RIGHT JOB

| REPORTED SYMPTOMS | LIKELY DIAGNOSIS | SUGGESTED REMEDY |
|---|---|---|
| | References unsuitable? | Change names of referees |
| | Unfit at insurance medical? | Check out with GP as soon as possible |
| | Fail positive vetting? | Not much to be done at this stage! |
| | Talked yourself out of the job? | Seek professional career choice and job search counselling |
| 9. Unable to agree suitable starting salary, etc. | Poor technique in negotiating contract of employment? | Seek professional career choice and job search counselling |
| 10. Withdraw from new job before agreed starting date | Change of heart? Unwilling to risk leap into unknown? | Lack of self-understanding Seek professional career choice and counselling |
| 11. Fail to complete satisfactory probationary period | Organization identifies incompatibility between you and the organization You identify incompatibility between your expectations and organization in practice | Bind up your wounds and summon up the courage to start again Count yourself fortunate that incompatibility has emerged soon after starting |
| 12. Complete satisfactory probation but leave in less than one year | You have failed to find job satisfaction despite giving the job every chance | No shame or stigma attaches when you have given the job a fair chance |

### David's story

David had spent more than 15 years in the same, junior admin. job with Ford Motor Company before recognizing that he was being left behind in the jobs race. His colleagues, nearly all new graduates, were clearly moving ahead much faster than him. He didn't resent their progress but bitterly regretted having abandoned his own further education. It was now too late.

Married with two young daughters and a burdensome mortgage, David decided he must compete internally for a more demanding and better-paid job and was soon successful in securing what he thought might be just the job.

Within 10 days of that internal transfer, David found the stressful demands of the new job more than he could take. He asked for his old job back—but it was filled.

Fearing he might languish in limbo, David resigned from Ford and found himself a job with another company, well within his ability range. But it involved long daily commuting or a house move. The compounded stress of daily travel, the prospect of domestic upheaval and coping with the new job got him down and he was soon clinically depressed on extended sick leave.

David and his new employers agreed that his probationary period was not satisfactory. In considerable desperation, David's wife then contacted his first boss at Ford, begging the company to allow David to return in however humble a capacity. His boss agreed to this on compassionate grounds. But it took several years for David to recover from his mistakes. 20 years on, he is still with Ford.

## SUGGESTIONS FOR FURTHER READING

H. Connor and G. Prior-Wandesford: *The Graduate Milk-Round: Its Changing Role and Pattern of Use*, Brighton: Institute of Manpower Studies (1984).

P. Herriot 'Graduate Recruitment: Psychological Contract and the Balance of Power' in *British Journal of Guidance and Counselling*, Vol 16 (1988) p 288.

The Central Services Unit of the Graduate Employment Service produces various useful free publications—e.g.

*Roget* – the annual Register of Graduate Employment and Training (and its Scottish counterpart ROGETSCOT).

*Forward Vacancies* – published fortnightly during Autumn and Spring terms.

S. D. Pearce: *The graduate connection: a guide to graduate recruitment*, Cambridge: CRAC (by) Hobson's Press (1976).

A. J. Raban: *Working in the European Communities: a guide for graduate recruiters and job-seekers*. Cambridge: CRAC (by) Hobson's Press (1988).

# The recruitment and selection process

*The successful attainment of an occupation could well be the
result of two sets of choices—a choice made by the individual
and a choice made by social institutions—implying that
people not only select occupations but are selected for
occupations.*

Stuart Timperley: *Personnel Planning and
Occupational Choice*

Chapter 10 tries to do three things:

1. To offer an overview of the recruitment and selection
   process.
2. To explain how Selectors choose the 'best' candidate.
3. To suggest how to improve your chances of being
   selected—and how to cope with rejection.

# THE EMPLOYER'S VIEWPOINT

One of the best ways to demystify any management function is to examine it not from the user's or client's viewpoint but from the inside—from the viewpoint of the manager or employer. Once you've taken a closer look at the recruitment and selection process from the employer's viewpoint, you'll understand more clearly:

1. How most employers manage the employment process.
2. How they reach their decisions once the interviews are over.

You should also be able to anticipate better the type of questions you may be asked at interview and so plan in advance how you'll respond to such questions.

First, how do job vacancies arise in the first place? In all sorts of ways: through expansion or evolution of the organization, through natural wastage and replacement of existing staff; and so on. Progressive employers don't advertise job vacancies without a great deal of forethought: Is this a *real* job? Does it *have* to be filled? Could we amalgamate *two existing jobs*? How and where do we find a field of *well-qualified candidates*? These questions form part of the regular checklist used by organizations which have adopted a progressive approach to *human resource planning*—a term which has been used for decades in the US and which has been more widely adopted in the UK since the Institute of Personnel Management published its *Statement on Human Resource Planning* in the mid-1980s. The Statement makes clear that:

> The term human resource planning has been used rather than the more traditional term 'manpower planning' to indicate that planning the people side of the business involves more than demand/supply balancing. Human resource plans should encompass the widest range of personnel policies and cover as many aspects of managing people as necessary to achieve the longer term objectives of the organization, with an emphasis on the effectiveness and costs of people.[1]

Once the vacancy has been authorized by senior management, the Personnel Manager will normally consult with appropriate members of Line Management before preparing two essential documents:

[1] Institute of Personnel Management: *Statement on Human Resource Planning*, London: IPM (1985).

- *A Job Specification* (or *Job Spec*) which provides, under six or seven headings, an indicative listing, but not an exhaustive catalogue, of the principal job demands. These may include:
  - (a) position to which the job-holder reports;
  - (b) whether required to deputise;
  - (c) number of persons supervised;
  - (d) size of budget, if any;
  - (e) reporting responsibilities.

- *A Personnel Specification* (or *Person Spec*) which sets out the qualifications, experience and personal qualities which an ideal candidate should possess. The Person Spec frequently follows a Seven Point Plan—a listing of personal attributes developed some years ago by the National Institute of Industrial Psychology—still highly favoured by many Selectors:
  - (1) *Physique*—including any disabilities or limitations.
  - (2) *Attainments*—educational and other achievements.
  - (3) *General intelligence*—a broad index of mental capacity.
  - (4) *Special aptitudes*—e.g. for mathematics, art, music, etc.
  - (5) *Interests*—leisure and other non-work pursuits.
  - (6) *Disposition*—temperament or personality traits.
  - (7) *Circumstances*—family, social or other considerations.

Management decisions must also be taken on whether—and, if so, where, when and how—to advertise the vacancy (display versus discreet; do-it-ourselves versus using recruitment and/or advertising consultants; one-to-one versus panel interviews). This tedious but critical, detailed preparation takes place long before the job advertisement eventually appears.

Let's suppose that the alluring advertisement which results from this preparation catches your attention and you decide to send for more details. In due course, you submit your application plus your CV, well before the closing date, and settle down to wait patiently for some kind of response.

## THE WINNOWING PROCESS

Back at the organization, the Personnel Manager sets up his administrative procedures and begins to line up the members of his interview panel. Then along comes your application, in the form of your CV plus a crisp cover letter—along with two hundred others! There's clearly a need for some 'winnowing' process to separate the 'wheat' from the 'chaff'. Applications are therefore subjected to a *primary screening* into three piles: (i) include; (ii) exclude; and (iii) maybe. There are three critical guidelines to this primary screening:

- *First, does this candidate appear genuinely qualified?* Does the application meet all the essential requirements of the job as shown in the Job Spec—the MUSTS? If not, exclude.

- *Second, is this candidate's application inherently credible?* Does the application reveal significant negative tendencies—the NOTS? If so, exclude

- *Third, does the candidate appear to be really interesting?* Does the application suggest desirable though non-essential qualities—the WANTS? If so, include.

An additional reason for this *primary screening*—normally undertaken by the Personnel Manager—is to reduce an excessively large total number of applications (say, 200) to manageable proportions by producing a *Long List* (say, 20 or 10% of total applications received), suitable for presentation to Line Management. During the process of review and discussion with Line Management, this Long List is then subjected to a *secondary screening* and rapidly reduced to a *Short List* ('Short Leet' in Scotland). It is this short-listing which brings you your invitation to initial panel interview.

## RECRUITMENT AND SELECTION: THE WINNOWING PROCESS

Eight important points are worth noting about recruitment and selection:

1. It is essentially a winnowing process—a management exercise in lawful discrimination.
2. The employer's first task is to attract as large a field of well-qualified candidates as possible. But he cannot know in advance how many valid applications a job advertisement will produce.
3. The employer's second task is to reduce too large a field of candidates to more manageable proportions, by excluding candidates whose applications show them to be unqualified, marginally qualified, invalid or uninteresting.
4. Poorly-presented CVs, incoherent applications and illegible letters are usually

excluded at this first stage. Your application and CV must both be immaculate to get you through to that vital initial interview.

**5.** The employer's third task is to keep the second list of candidates ('Maybes') to one side in case the first list ('Includes') fails to produce an appointable candidate.

**6.** The employer's fourth task is to invite candidates for initial interview.

**7.** Whether the Line Manager or Personnel Manager presides over the interview panel, the important roles of the Chairman are to see fair play, to keep the interview going at a brisk pace along the right lines with every Selector having an opportunity to pose some questions.

**8.** Finally, there is the crucial task of inviting panel members to discuss their assessments of the different candidates in order to arrive at a decision on the one who meets most of the selection criteria and who should therefore be offered the job.

Every employment interview produces an irreducible minimum level of stress amongst the candidates—and even amongst some selectors! If you arrive much too early for interview, you may have a long wait and simply add to your own stress. If you arrive too late, however, you may disqualify yourself from interview altogether—unless you can phone to say you've been struck down by flu or a taxi and would like to reschedule your interview.

### Horatio's story

A friend of mine — let's call him Horatio — once arrived more than an hour late for a crucial interview. He felt very bad about this because he was suffering from a stye in one eye at the time and felt very self-conscious wearing an eyepatch.

Imagine his surprise when he was warmly greeted by the Personnel Manager, who had apparently lost an eye in the Second World War— and was also wearing an eyepatch! We all need a lucky break from time to time — Horatio decided this was his!

PS: He didn't get the job.

With admirable tact, you arrive for your interview just in time. You are ushered into the interview room. You look good but feel rotten: short of sleep, dry mouth syndrome, headache. There are four, five, six hands to shake and names to remember. What are these Selectors looking for? The same things—or different things? To whom should you appeal—if anybody?

In his new book on interviewing, Dr David Lewis recommends interview candidates to establish good eye contact with all members of the interview panel immediately upon entering the interview room. As Dr Lewis says:

You never get a second chance to make a first impression.[2]

Like it or not, research shows that most Selectors judge candidates in less than 4 minutes—by their appearance, their voices, and their initial response to questions. Dull, boring or erratic candidates are normally thanked politely for coming and tactfully sent on their way. Sharp, flashy, self-promoting candidates may be lucky enough to be humoured. Bright but reticent candidates may be given time to thaw out. Post-experience candidates are mostly hired on the strength of their proven track-record; new graduates for their potential rather than their academic or other achievements. Sensible Selectors rarely waste time on others.

Let's assume that there's nothing to choose between the final group of candidates in terms of their technical qualifications alone. What other *specific personal qualities* are Selectors generally looking for, to help them narrow their choice? Despite the almost infinite detailed variations in Job Specs and Person Specs, there are *six key qualities* which impress most Selectors when they make judgements about candidates:

- 1. *Self-confidence*—which is closely linked to self-awareness of strengths and limitations.

- 2. *Vitality*—'psychic energy' or that inner glow or personal 'sparkle'.

- 3. *Initiative*—the capacity to be a self-starter, not a robot waiting to be programmed.

- 4. *Sensitivity*—the ability to work successfully with others as a fully fledged member of the team.

- 5. *Integrity*—the capacity to distinguish moral from immoral conduct and the ability to prefer the first to the second. Either you've got it or you haven't. There's no way you can fake it!

- 6. *Communication skills*—the ability to relate to other people in speech, writing and non-verbal ways—which includes letting the Selectors know just how hungry you are for the job.

[2] David Lewis: *The Secret Language of Success*, London: Bantam (1989).

## THREE GOLDEN INTERVIEW RULES

When all's said and done, there are really only three golden rules to help you through employment interviews:

* *First, be positive.*

Whatever you've done in your life, try to describe it positively, if at all possible. Selectors are only human. They can't help being psychologically prejudiced in favour of candidates who appear strongly positive in their answers to questions and their general attitudes; and equally prejudiced against candidates who appear negative.

* *Second, be honest.*

It generally pays to be honest in life—and it's often much easier than lying! But telling the truth doesn't mean you need to tell the *whole* truth—even if you knew it. If you don't know the answer to a question, why not say so? You'd be surprised how many weak or dishonest candidates think they can flannel their way through interviews. Why not demonstrate your maturity, by being honest about yourself?

* *Third, be yourself.*

If you don't have the relevant experience, it's no use pretending that you do. You won't be able to handle the follow-up. On the other hand, *do* let the selectors know that you learn fast. Self-confidence comes from self-knowledge—your strengths as well as your weaknesses. Even your failures can be made to yield invaluable self-knowledge.


## HOW DO SELECTORS MAKE THEIR FINAL DECISIONS?

Since this is *the key to the whole selection process*, you need to have a very clear understanding of how it generally works. In somewhat over-simplified terms, selection is a combined function of *exclusion* and *matching*. The whole process might be fairly described as being essentially as *an exercise in lawful discrimination*.

Selectors begin the complex process of selection by *excluding* problematic candidates—i.e. those who reveal 'contrary indications' in their written applications, or their CVs, or their interview responses—including their body-language (or non-verbal communication)—all of which give clues to their unsuitability. Picking your teeth, cleaning your ears, continuous plucking of your hair, or clenching your bloodless hands in front of you throughout the interview might all be detrimental to your chances of being selected. It's plainly impossible to provide an exhaustive list of 'contrary indications', because they vary with the Selectors. But they include any one or more of five indicators.

## WHAT REDUCES YOUR CREDIBILITY AT INTERVIEW?

— Anything which simply doesn't 'add up' about you.
— Anything which undermines a Selector's confidence in your ability to do the job.
— Anything which throws doubt on your qualifications or relevant experience.
— Anything which questions your 'intelligence-in-action', your capacity to relate successfully to others, to learn on your feet, to 'pick up the ball and run'.
— Any evidence which reduces your credibility as a successful employee may result in your being excluded as a candidate for the job.

Having excluded as many marginal candidates as possible and thereby reduced the final choice to two or three candidates, Selectors proceed to the *'mix-and-match'* stage. They compare and contrast their individual assessments of the surviving candidates to discover which of them produces *the closest matches to the Job Spec and the Person Spec*, bearing in mind the vital need to maintain a balance or 'mix' of different types of personality, age and experience within the work team. Sensible Selectors try to avoid 'cloning'—i.e. selecting candidates who virtually replicate the characteristics of existing staff. Strength in a work team comes not from uniformity but from a well-matched diversity of team members.

If the complex process of advertising, primary screening, long-listing, secondary screening, short-listing, interviewing and post-interview discussion have all been reasonably effective, the Selectors should now have relatively little difficulty in deciding which of the surviving candidates represents the 'best match' for the vacancy they wish to fill. If none of the remaining candidates comes up to the standard specified in the Job Spec and Person Spec, Selectors may decide *not* to make an offer of employment but to re-advertise or to defer filling the post.

Conversely, if there are two or more unusually well-qualified candidates left to choose from, the Selectors may have some protracted—even agonized—discussion ahead of them, before they finally reach a decision. *The job is normally offered to the 'best' candidate—i.e. the one who comes closest to fulfilling all the MUSTS and as many of the weighted WANTS as possible.*

*Finally*, wise and experienced Selectors never reject their second or third-best candidates until the 'best' candidate has signified acceptance of the offer of employment. It's worth recalling that recruitment and selection is inevitably an emotional as well as a rational two-way process—with candidates free to exercise their own independent judgement on whether or not they wish to accept an employment offer. The 'best' candidate may decide after reflection to reject the offer, or may attempt to negotiate an improved salary or fringe-benefit package which the employer is not willing or able to concede (see Chapter 14). So, even if you're convinced you were *not* the brightest or 'best' candidate on the day, you may still be in with a chance! Remember, there's many a slip 'twixt cup and lip'—and many a 'second-best' candidate has finally emerged triumphant at the end of a protracted recruitment and selection process.

## HOW DO YOU COPE WITH INTERVIEW REJECTION?

You'll know the feeling. You thought you did really well at interview. You appeared keen but not desperate. You gave just the right answers. You were self-confident and knowledgeable without appearing coy or cocky. Then along comes this awful rejection letter. A nasty sour feeling in the pit of your stomach. They probably don't deserve you anyway. Or perhaps your interview answers were not as acceptable as you first thought?

Either way, you didn't get the job. So, what do you do now? Go off and sulk? Pick yourself up, brush yourself down, and start all over again? We suggest you first take stock. True, you didn't get the job. The real question is: Did you get the most out of the experience?

Think about it this way. Every interview, successful or otherwise, provides a unique learning opportunity: how to improve your self-image; how to improve your self-projection; how to handle interview questions with greater aplomb. You can learn to cope better with rejection by carrying out an intelligent interview post-mortem. This way, you increase your self-knowledge and self-confidence for your next interview—the one that really matters now.

### TEN QUESTIONS FOR YOUR POST-INTERVIEW CHECKLIST

1. *Did the interview go the way I expected?*
Where were you under-prepared or vulnerable? Jot down the questions—and the gist of your answers, before you forget. Of course, you handled some questions better than others. It's the areas of weakness you need to concentrate on now.

2. *Did I show them I really wanted the job?*
Employers are always looking for well-directed enthusiasm. Did you keep yours hidden? Or was it all over the place?

3. *Did I do my homework?*
Employers are impressed when you show that you've researched the organization. It shows that you really care.

4. *Did I understand what the interviewer was getting at?*
You must learn to decode interview questions to get at 'the music behind the words'—and 'the words behind the music'.

5. *Did I 'sell' myself short?*
You know you were well-qualified for the job, but did you tell them?

6. *Did I suggest how my skills might help the organization solve its problems— or was I pre-occupied with my own?*
Employers are not in the charity business. They hire staff primarily to help them improve their performance by raising productivity or profitability. Employee benefits take second place.

7. *Did I hook the job in the first half of the interview but fail to land it in the second half?*
Some candidates don't know how to speak up. Others don't know when to shut up! You need to speak up for yourself, certainly. But you must not over-sell yourself. The employer needs to need you more than you need him.

8. *Did I have unrealistic expectations about this interview?*
It's not unknown for candidates to apply for jobs they don't really want—and to be interviewed for jobs they aren't really qualified to do.

9. *Did I think of some of my best answers on the way out?*
The French call it *l'esprit de l'escalier*—staircase wit. That suggests you need better preparation and more interview practice.

10. *Did you have questions ready to ask them?*
Employers almost invariably give you the chance to ask questions yourself. Remember, they judge you by the range and quality of your questions—as well as your answers!

In short, whilst taking stock of your last (unsuccessful) interview, you're preparing yourself intelligently for your next (hopefully more successful) interview. In that way, you make every interview count. Nothing is wasted. There's certainly no time for self-pity or regrets. *Non. Rien de rien.*

Finally, you can always try to get in touch with the organization and ask the Chairman of the interview panel in confidence why you didn't get the job. Don't be surprised if you're fed soft-soap. It may be better to get professional interview advice and see yourself on closed-circuit TV.

## SUGGESTIONS FOR FURTHER READING

Institute of Personnel Management: *Statement on Human Resource Planning*, London: IPM (1985).

Derek Torrington and Laura Hall: *Personnel Management: A New Approach*. London: Prentice-Hall (1987), Chapters 14–16.

David Lewis: *The Secret Language of Success*. London: Bantam (1989).

# Decoding job ads and submitting job applications

*SECOND MILLENIUM BANK seeks experienced young Economist to work on Strategic Analysis in its newly-established International Portfolio Management Division. Outstanding opportunity for exceptionally qualified candidate to join the Bank at an important stage of its development. Please address current CV to: John P. Hampton, Personnel Manager, Second Millenium Bank, 300 Aldersgate, London EC2 9KT*

Chapter 11 tries to do three things:

1. To explain how to decode a job advertisement.
2. To analyse the process of applying for a job.
3. To suggest ways to improve your job applications.

Do you know the cost of a single display advertisement for a typical middle-grade management job vacancy? To take just one example: *The Daily Telegraph*'s current charge (October 1989) for a *single* display advertisement, of the kind shown in the headquote to this chapter, amounts to £500 plus VAT. Even the largest multinationals, with the most generous personnel recruitment budgets, must economize in their use of space when advertising job vacancies—hence the abbreviations, the conventional signs and the cryptic language used by many employers (and their advertising agencies) when they *encode* job advertisements (job ads).

Let's begin to *decode* or 'unpack' the ad in the headquote above to see how much we can learn about the job, the employer and how we might approach our own job application—always assuming we still want the job when we've found out more about it!

- **First, who's the advertiser?**
Perhaps you've never heard of the Second Millenium Bank? If the job nevertheless sounds attractive, you should research the bank at your nearest college or municipal library. Read the bank's last two Annual Reports and Accounts. Check the *Financial Times*' Index for articles on the bank's current development plans and its new International Division. Try to find out the name of the Division Manager. If you decide to pursue your interest, phone the bank's Public Relations Department, ask for the information you need and request that they send you a background information pack on the bank in general and its International Division in particular.

- **Second, what's the job about?**
If you need more technical information about the work of the International Portfolio Management Division of a major bank, start by doing some basic reading in the library—if only to have some questions in mind, then make direct contact with the Information Office of another, possibly a rival, bank. Tell them you're speaking from your University or College Library and that you need some information about the bank for research purposes (all perfectly true and above board). Needless to say, you don't need to mention your interest in the Second Millenium vacancy. Wherever possible, ask the bank whether they would be willing to get one of their younger members of staff in the International Portfolio Management Division to call you back and/or to send you any non-classified documentation

(such as a Divisional Manager's Report on the last year's operations). Banks and other business houses generally take the view that these constitute legitimate enquiries from members of the investing public and usually have a sizeable budget from which to meet the cost of such enquiries.

- **Third, what are they really looking for?**
Banks use words with precision. When a bank's job ad specifies an 'experienced young Economist' and an 'exceptionally qualified candidate', they must have some ideal qualifications and qualities in mind. What are they really after? And how far do you measure up to those ideals?

First, note they're asking for candidates with a professional training in Economics rather than in Banking. That tells us something. Second, they want candidates to be both young and experienced. That implies at least 5 years' relevant experience post-graduation—which brings us to the age range 28–30.

An 'exceptionally qualified candidate' presumably means qualified either academically or practically—and preferably both. If you've completed no further training since graduation, you may be under-qualified. But if it's qualification through excellent practical experience they're after, you may still be in with a chance. Why not give Mr Hampton's office a phone call and discuss the point informally? Directory Enquiries will give you his London office number. You should ask for him by name but be ready to discuss the matter with any other member of his staff.

The job ad implies that the bank needs a young Economist to start work immediately in the newly-created Division. Has it advertised the post before now? If so, why has it failed to attract a suitable applicant so far? It's not difficult to see why no starting salary or fringe-benefit package is mentioned in the ad. Presumably there's no difficulty in offering an attractive employment package to a suitable candidate. However, be on your guard. You may be invited to interview as a genuine candidate in good faith—or simply as a make-weight candidate to set against an already most-favoured (possibly internal) candidate. So, don't build your hopes too soon!

- **Fourth, how can you make your application outstanding?**
If you believe banks are essentially conservative institutions, you may decide to keep your application very clean, formal, factual and conventional. If, however, you decide, after some research, that they're opening an exciting new era in their International Division and are

looking for a more adventurous type of candidate, you might consider mentioning your Outward Bound qualification; or the fact that you once sailed down the Amazon in a dug-out canoe; or abseiled down the Matterhorn. And that your father was Polish and mother German—so that you speak fluent German and Polish. That might ensure you're called to that critical first interview! So, you now have much more to guide you when you sit down to revise your CV and to draft your job application.

## APPLYING FOR A JOB

The process of applying for a job, in response to a job ad, is not difficult to describe. The preparation of an effective and impressive job application, however, approaches a work of art—certainly a piece of creative craftsmanship. But it's an art or craft that can be learned and which every job hunter must master.

There are *three key stages* to submitting any job application, each stage having its own *tactical objective*:

- *Stage 1*: Finding some direct linkage(s) between the advertised job and your present qualifications, experience, etc.

- *Stage 2*: Drafting your application in an appropriate form of words which does justice to the strength of your qualifications, experience, etc.

- *Stage 3*: Cutting your application down to size to remove any surplus words or irrelevant material.

**Stage 1 Objective: To establish your credibility as a candidate**
This should not be too difficult—provided that:

1.  You've successfully decoded the job ad.
2.  You've decided you still want the job.
3.  You are reasonably well qualified for it.
4.  You're strongly motivated to pursue the application and committed to see the selection process through to its conclusion—successful or otherwise.

Incidentally, the third proviso doesn't necessarily mean you've wide or deep experience in *every* aspect of the job to be filled. There's rarely an ideal candidate who can provide that perfect combination of qualifications. But you must establish your overall credibility by showing that you have a winning combination of:

○ 1.   Some directly relevant experience which you can adapt and bring to bear in the advertised post.

○ 2.   The capacity to learn fast and so make an immediate and increasingly valuable contribution in helping the employer to solve his problems.

That's going to take some doing—especially since your letter of application must be kept fairly brief!

**Stage 2 Objective: To arouse the curiosity of the Selectors and so make them want to learn more about you**

This can be burdensome or relatively easy—depending on whether you've had enough practice at it—and whether or not you've mastered the use of a word processor. The chore about drafting anything is that *you begin by getting much of it wrong. You then get it as right as possible* by revising your first draft, and then revising that, until you finally arrive at something which approximates to what you wanted to say in the first place. That process can take hours or days—even weeks—except that you don't have the luxury of such delay. There's always the danger that you may lose heart or miss the final submission date. *Instead of striving to make your job application perfect, you should aim instead to make it perfectly acceptable.*

That's where the word processor comes into its own. If you've never used one, you're in for a wonderful surprise. Without hyperbole, the word processor is one of the marvels of modern microtechnology! It has utterly transformed this author's life—and his fortunes!

If you *don't* type, you may draft in pencil, pen or biro on the alternate lines of your paper. As you revise your draft, you fit your revised wording between the lines, until you fill them completely and need to start again with a clean sheet of paper.

If you *do* type, you draft your application by typing in double-spaced format and again revise between the lines. But it's sometimes difficult to line up the revisions and the existing first draft—and sooner or later you must load a fresh piece of paper into the typewriter.

*If you do use a word processor,* however, you already know how easy it is. You type your first rough draft, which is then saved in the memory of the machine. You now have two choices:

○ 1. To print your first draft and use that as the basis for manuscript revision—which can then be used to edit or revise the first draft, retrieved from the memory store.

○ 2. To revise directly from your first rough draft, without bothering to print intermediate drafts.

But whereas with a traditional typewriter you need to type a fresh version every time you amend your draft—e.g. altering the sequence of words or sentences—with a word processor you simply instruct the machine to rearrange the existing text for you. No sweat!

Whether you draft using word processor, electronic typewriter, electric typewriter, traditional typewriter, biro, pencil, pen or even old-fashioned quill—you should try to keep all the numbered versions of your successive drafts. There are three good reasons for suggesting you do this:

○ *First*, you'll have a record of how much better your final acceptable draft is compared with your first or intermediate drafts.

○ *Second*, you'll have a permanent reminder why it's worth persevering with editing or redrafting future job applications.

○ *Third*, you'll be able to analyse the kind of changes you make in successive drafts—and so save yourself the future trouble of going through each stage.

**Stage 3 Objective: To present yourself to the Selectors in as attractive a manner as possible**

This stage can be extremely tricky because you've struggled to put across all your key selling points in one letter—only to find you're now called upon to prune the overall length to keep the final typed or hand-written version within some artificially prescribed limits—no more than, say, one side of a sheet of notepaper. That limit alone might suggest you use a typewriter in preference to a hand-written application. But there's more to it than that, as we shall see.

Pruning is never easy. You have to make cuts of the right length at just the right places—or the result will be a misshapen mess. Here are a few hints:

○ Treat your job application letter as if you were personally paying to send every word you write by telegram to Melbourne or Los Angeles.

In a word, make every word count and not a word surplus to essential requirements.

○ Cut out everything which is self-evident or contained in your accompanying CV.

○ Cross-refer to the CV if necessary but do not anticipate the content or impact of the CV itself—otherwise it may never be read!

○ Be courteous but not fulsome in your initial greeting and final salutation—and so save more words.

○ Do not cut out words which communicate your enthusiasm for the job and your commitment to the job application.

Having decided on your pruning, ask for somebody's help in checking and re-checking the final text of your application letter. You need a second person's help because you may miss errors in the application— simply because you tend to read what you expect to read—rather than what's actually been written.

To illustrate this drafting and editing process, given below are the first, second, third and final versions of a job application for the vacancy advertised in the headquote to this chapter. Note that, whilst the final version seems *perfectly acceptable* to this author, you might wish to make further revisions before you were satisfied with it.

## FIRST DRAFT VERSION OF A JOB APPLICATION

Dear Sir or Madam,

I am currently employed by the Midas Merchant Bank in London and have been looking around for a position of the kind which you advertised in the Financial Times last week. I have noticed with interest that you describe the job as 'Strategic Analyst' whereas I am currently employed as a Financial Analyst in the International Trade Section of the Bank. Nevertheless, I consider myself well qualified for the post by the fact of my first degree in Economics and my second qualification, an MBA with special interest in Financial Strategic Planning, which is my speciality.

I enclose a copy of my current curriculum vitae and look forward to hearing from you.

Yours sincerely

Job Hunter

**SECOND IMPROVED VERSION OF A JOB APPLICATION**

Dear Sir:

With reference to your advertisement in today's Financial Times for a Strategic Analyst, I should like to be considered as a candidate for this vacancy.

I am a graduate in Economics with an MBA in Financial Planning Strategy, currently employed as an International Financial Analyst with the Midas Merchant Bank.

I enclose a CV in support of my application.

Yours truly

Job Hunter


**THIRD MORE POLISHED VERSION OF A JOB APPLICATION**

The Personnel Manager

Strategic Analyst

I wish to offer myself as a candidate for the above-named post, advertised in The Financial Times on Wednesday, 10th August 1989.

Having spent the whole of my career since graduation with the Midas Merchant Bank, I'm now interested in making a significant career move. I believe I would bring relevant qualifications and directly relevant experience to the position you seek to fill. I enclose a copy of my current CV and should appreciate the opportunity of a meeting to discuss the vacancy further.

Yours sincerely

Job Hunter

**FINAL ACCEPTABLE VERSION OF JOB APPLICATION**

PERSONAL
Mr John P Hampton
Personnel Manager
Second Millenium Bank
300 Aldersgate
London EC2 9KT

Dear Mr Hampton:

Strategic Analyst

I wish to apply for this post, advertised in the *Financial Times* dated 10 August 1989.

For the past three years I have served as Personal Assistant to the Director of Strategic Financial Planning here at Midas Merchant Bank. Having recently completed a Postgraduate Diploma in Strategic Portfolio Management at the London Business School, I should like to learn more about how you propose to structure and operate your new International Portfolio Management Division.

In view of Second Millenium's current involvement in financial consultancy in Eastern Europe, I'm convinced that my command of German and Polish makes this an area of the bank's work in which I could make an outstanding contribution. I should therefore welcome the opportunity of an early interview to discuss the vacancy you seek to fill and to explain further my qualifications for the position.

Full details of my career are set out in the enclosed copy of my CV.

Yours sincerely

Job Hunter

## WAYS TO IMPROVE YOUR JOB APPLICATION

You want to make the best possible impression with your application. But you're in competition with many others, some perhaps better qualified than you. How do you make your application stand out in a crowded stack? Here are ten practical suggestions:

- **First, is your application attractive?**
  Put your application aside overnight and then try to approach it afresh, read it with new eyes—those of the Personnel Officer who will receive it.

  Does it have eye-appeal? Is it fresh, neat, and clearly laid out? Does it make you want to turn the page and read more? If you don't take the trouble to make your application look attractive, why should you expect your reader to find it attractive?

- **Second, is your application short and economical?**
  Does it make its points succinctly and effectively? Verbiage is the worst enemy of job applications. If the reader becomes quickly bored, your application could well be rejected at this early stage.

- **Third, is it substantial enough for the job vacancy?**
  Does your application carry weight? Does it provide sufficient evidence of your accomplishments to date, your qualifications, your competence and enthusiasm for the job?

  The more senior the job, the more you need to signal your achievements to date. The more junior the job, the more you need to talk about yourself—your potential and commitment to the type of job and organization you're applying for.

- **Fourth, does your application give hostages to fortune?**
  Try to avoid saying anything which might offend or cause a negative reaction in your reader and so put your application at unnecessary risk of being rejected. For example, you don't normally need to disclose which political party, religious affiliation or ethnic minority you belong to unless you feel it's absolutely essential to the success of your application.

  So, unless you're applying for a job as, say, Local Organizer of (a) the Labour Party, (b) the Methodist Conference, or (c) the Anti-Apartheid League—you don't need to say you're a socialist, a Christian or a black, respectively! Dare to be unique—but why take unnecessary risks?

- **Fifth, is the tone of your application positive throughout?**
  'Never apologize, never explain' may sound cynical—a sceptical view of life. And, in practice, of course, we may all have to do both. Nevertheless, you should try to keep your application as bright and positive as possible. Avoid the nuances and reservations at this early stage. There'll be plenty of time to add them later, if needed.

- **Sixth, does your application imply more than it says?**
  There's nothing wrong in trying unobtrusively to score additional points—for example by hinting or implying more than you actually say about your qualifications and experience for the vacancy. Arouse your reader's curiosity, by all means. But don't try to say everything there is to be said about yourself—thereby draining your application of any further curiosity value.

- **Seventh, is your application consistent?**
  If you write a letter of application for a job vacancy—and are then required to complete an application form,[1] do make sure the information you provide is factually consistent. If you feel the need for some stylistic variation, confine it to your supplementary material or comments, not essential factual data.

- **Eighth, don't send more material than you're asked for**
  If the application form asks you for your views on 'Salmonella: The Problem in an Eggshell'—or 'Chinese Junk Bond Markets'—you have few options—one of which is always to give up the application right there and then! If you're asked to send a recent passport-size photograph of yourself, comply precisely with the request. Don't send a holiday snap or a photograph of your wedding!

  The general rule is this: don't send unsolicited materials of any kind—no photographs, no birth certificates, no examples of your work, no references, no matter how glowing. In fact, the more glowing, the more suspicious they become. But if you're asked to provide the names of two referees, think carefully before you offer the names of people whose permission you've not yet obtained. They might just get an overnight request for a telephone reference. It's been known to happen!

- **Ninth, don't stint on the notepaper**
  Go without dinner, let the landlord wait for the rent, let somebody else buy the next round—but don't submit job applications on cheap and nasty notepaper. It doesn't need to be rag-based, hand-blocked or delicately perfumed. Equally, it should not be a page torn out of an exercise book or a sheet of continuous computer stationery. Word process your application, by all means—but then make sure you photocopy it neatly onto decent copy paper. Beware of using coloured notepaper! Many employers—both traditional and non-traditional—view coloured notepaper with suspicion. It has even been suggested

---

[1] For further advice on completing Application Forms, see below.

that the use of coloured notepaper reveals either a phoney artistic temperament or a desperate attempt to grab attention—even sexual perversion!

- **Tenth, try to co-ordinate the format, style and content of your application**
  If you're writing to a business house, make sure your letter is businesslike. If you're applying for a job in the British Civil Service, complete your application form in black ink and ensure that everything you write is accurate, detailed, unemotional. Conversely, if you're applying for a job as Copywriter at a leading London agency, choose an exciting colour of notepaper, write a letter in your own boldest handwriting, and don't be afraid to let it all hang out. The style, content and appearance of your letter will be taken to reflect your creativity and will therefore be judged as an example of your work—as the following vibrant example from the US clearly demonstrates!

**I've worked hard to reach you,<br>but I'll work even harder<br>once you reach me.**

---

*All your hear today is that no one hires people straight out of college. And I think I know why. No experience, right?*

*Wrong. Any good agency knows that experience is where you find it, not how long you've worked in the business.*

*And that's precisely why I chose your agency. Along with producing on-target, result-oriented advertising for your clients, you're one of the few agencies today who know how to take advantage of opportunities, whether it's a new account or a potential employee.*

*So let me get to the point. Quite simply, I want a career with your agency, not just a job.*

*But why you in particular? Because we're very much alike. You see, I've managed to take advantage of my opportunities. While others looked for easy courses to fulfill many of their degree requirements, I took the equivalent of a minor in business, primarily for the intensive marketing background I knew I would need. And while others created 'pretend' advertising in our advertising courses, I produced results, such as the campaign I created for the USC Campus Alcohol Project which is now being used successfully throughout many southeastern colleges and universities.*

*Although my resumé tells the rest, it doesn't spell out one important thing! I'm ready, eager and able to start producing results for your agency.*
*All I need now is the chance.*

Robert J. Gugliemo

Source: A. Jerome Jewler: *Creative Strategy in Advertising*, Belmont, California: Wadsworth Publishing Company (1985), Chapter 14: 'Breaking Into Advertising', p. 222.

## COMPLETING APPLICATION FORMS

When applying for some job vacancies, you'll be invited to complete and return an Application Form. This may initially appear straightforward or boring insofar as the questions call for factual information under a dozen or so headings. Even so, you need to be meticulous in supplying accurate information on which you may be asked questions at interview. It pays to photocopy the blank form and prepare a rough draft of your answers before completing the final version in ink. *Always retain* a photocopy of the final version submitted.

In some cases, you may be asked questions which require more thought and some research—even though the information required is still factual. For example, the Application Form for a leading electronics multinational (anonymous) includes the following 15 sections:

### THE XYZ COMPANY: APPLICATION FORM

| | | |
|---|---|---|
| 1. | PERSONAL DATA | Please supply full names, address, etc. |
| 2. | EMPLOYMENT HISTORY | Please give full details |
| 3. | EDUCATION | Please provide full information from secondary school onwards |
| 4. | REFERENCES | Please provide three business references or academic/professional referees (if no previous employment) |
| 5. | MOBILITY<br>Willing to travel? | Extensively (60–75%)<br>Occasionally<br>Not at all |

Willing to relocate?            Yes/No
                                 If yes, any limitations or restrictions?

6.  ORGANIZATIONS to which you belong
    Social
    Civic
    Professional

7.  OTHER INTERESTS            Include athletics, hobbies or other outside interests

8.  LEADERSHIP                 List all positions of responsibility and leadership

9.  ACHIEVEMENTS               Include all accomplishments, activities, honours and
                               awards

10. ACCOMPLISHMENTS            Describe your single most significant
                               accomplishment during employment or education

11. CAREER OBJECTIVE           Give a specific and concise statement

12. SECURITY INFORMATION       The nature of our business requires strict security
                               standards. The following information is required.

(i)   Previous address              (ii)  For how long?
(iii) Any other last names used     (iv)  National Insurance No.
(v)   Passport No.                  (vi)  Expiry date
(vii) Have you ever been convicted of a crime?
      If yes, please provide details of offence, place, result and date
(viii) Has a security clearance ever been refused or cancelled?
      If yes, please explain
(ix)  Spouse's occupation           (x)   Spouse's employer

13. HEALTH                     The Company Health Benefit Plan covers pre-
                               existing and/or manifest conditions one year from
                               the effective date of coverage.

Tick each of the following conditions which you, your spouse or dependent children now
have or have ever had.

| Condition | You | Spouse | Child | Last Treatment Date |
|---|---|---|---|---|
| Arthritis, Bursitis, Rheumatism | | | | |
| Asthma, Bronchitis | | | | |
| Back Trouble | | | | |
| Bladder or Prostate Trouble | | | | |
| ▷ Bunions or Foot Problems | | | | |

124

| Condition | You | Spouse | Child | Last Treatment | Date |
|---|---|---|---|---|---|
| Cancer, Cysts, Tumours | | | | | |
| Diabetes | | | | | |
| Drug/Alcohol Problems | | | | | |
| Epilepsy or Nervous Condition | | | | | |
| Female Disorders | | | | | |
| Gall Bladder Problems | | | | | |
| Heart Disease | | | | | |
| Haemorrhoids or Rectal Trouble | | | | | |
| Hernia | | | | | |
| High/Low Blood Pressure | | | | | |
| Kidney Stones or Urinary Condition | | | | | |
| Mental Condition | | | | | |
| Psychological Counselling | | | | | |
| Severe Headaches | | | | | |
| Stomach or Intestinal Condition | | | | | |
| Tuberculosis | | | | | |
| Varicose Veins | | | | | |
| Any Other Condition or Injury | | | | | |
| If other, explain | | | | | |

If these conditions do not apply to you or
your dependants, write 'None'

How much time have you lost from work in
the past year?
Please explain

Do you now or have you ever smoked?
If yes, provide dates, quantity and type
(cigarettes, cigar, pipe, etc.)

Indicate your current status:
Smoker        Non-smoker

Name and address of your doctor

14. ADDITIONAL INFORMATION IN SUPPORT OF YOUR APPLICATION
    Add anything you wish on this page in support of your application.

15. DECLARATION

    I declare that the answers given herein are complete and true to the best of my knowledge
    and belief. I understand that any misrepresentation or omission may preclude an offer of
    employment, lead to a withdrawal of such an offer or lead to my employment being
    terminated. I authorize investigation of all statements made by me and understand that
    consideration for employment is contingent upon satisfactory reference checks.

    Signed:                                    Date:

This application will remain active for 30 days

Most of these questions should present no difficulty. But how should you deal with some of the more personal or intrusive questions? There are some pitfalls here worth considering briefly. You should obviously seek to keep your replies as factual and accurate as possible. But how should you deal, for example, with *ORGANIZATIONS*? Suppose you played trombone in The Salvation Army in Swindon? Or were once a fully paid-up member of the Croydon Social and Liberal Democrats? Or the Kentish Town Young Socialists? You might decide to declare the latter—but what about the former? Or vice versa?

Or let's take *OTHER INTERESTS*? It's one thing to say you won a Half-Blue for Tennis or Rugby at Oxford or Cambridge. What if you were the Captain of Table Tennis? Or Tiddleywinks? Or Tortoise Races? Or founder member of the University of Sheffield Speleological Society? Yes, that still sounds impressive. If you were an office-bearer or a prize-winner, it's probably worth including. If it was simply a personal matter, leave it out.

What about *LEADERSHIP*? If you carried off an inscribed Silver Salver as Student Debater of the Year 1990, or were Principal Flautist in the University of Edinburgh Chamber Orchestra, that's fine. (But perhaps they're best listed under *ACHIEVEMENTS rather than LEADERSHIP*?) Of if you led the Glasgow College of Art's near-disastrous White-Water Rafting Trip down the Colorado River? Or the University of Bath Business School's alcoholic investigation into Historical Accounting Practices at the Hospice de Beaune, in Burgundy? Yes, they were undoubtedly leadership roles—however well or badly you filled them. So they're certainly worth listing. But what if your only significant leadership role was organizing the Basildon College of Further Education's disastrous Day Trip to Southend-on-Sea on the last, rain-swept Saturday in August 1990, when a member of staff was 'accidentally' pushed off a breakwater and drowned? Discretion may be the better part of Leadership — so, leave it out.

So we come to *ACCOMPLISHMENTS*. Suppose you have nothing to report? It's one thing to acquire a virtue which you lack, but how do you instantly accomplish anything worth reporting? The question invites you to select 'your single most significant accomplishment' from amongst many! Clearly, you should set your sights modestly. What about your degree result? Achieving a Lower Second Class Honours despite having flu symptoms, just when you've split up a beautiful friendship — and done little or no academic work for three years—surely that's something of an accomplishment?

*CAREER OBJECTIVE* is a tricky subject, especially when you're asked to give a specific and concise statement. A brief statement along the following lines might be better than attempting to fill all 20 lines provided for your answer:

> My initial objective is to make an early entry into the Research and Development Department of a major electronics multinational and, if possible, to continue my practical work on diffusion problems associated with argon semi-conductors. Thereafter, I should like to spend some time working with counterpart researchers in the United States to learn all I can about advanced industrial management techniques with a view to leading my own research team within a period of five years.

Finally, there's that entire blank page simply headed *ADDITIONAL INFORMATION IN SUPPORT OF YOUR APPLICATION*. What on earth do you say? I'd be surprised if you haven't thoroughly ransacked and exhausted your entire fund of life experience long before you reach this final section. Now you see why it's important to complete a draft version of the Application Form before you commit pen to paper. You need to rationalize your spread of information over the completed form—and ensure that it's consistent throughout. Perhaps you'd care to draft something along the following lines for this final section:

> From my early schooldays, I've been engrossed by electrical/electronic gadgetry. I built my first transistorized radio before I was twelve, albeit with some help from my aunt, who's Senior Lecturer in Applied Physics at Hatfield Polytechnic. Since 1980, I've regularly attended the annual meetings of British Association for the Advancement of Science and presented a 1987 paper on Double-Laminated Transistors in the Junior Science Section.
>
> Despite my wide-ranging interests in applied science, my principal ambition is to work in advanced electronics to enable me to match my theoretical knowledge with practical experience and so select an appropriate subject area for a Doctoral thesis on the application of transistors in electronic components.
>
> I should therefore welcome the opportunity to discuss these aims at my employment interview and to learn how I might make an early contribution to the work of your Research Department.

Finally, note the important *Declaration* which provides the company with the lawful basis for investigating your personal life without further warning—even though you're still only completing an initial Application Form. You might ask yourself whether you still want to work for a company which requires you to sign such an open-ended Declaration!

Good luck with completing your Application Forms! Remember to *sign and date the final Declaration! And do take a copy for your file.*

## SUGGESTIONS FOR FURTHER READING

CRAC, *Graduate Employment and Training*, Cambridge: Hobsons Publishing (annually).

GO, *Graduate Opportunities*, London: Newpoint Publishing (annually).

# Preparing an immaculate CV

*They tell it from here to Thermopylae:*
*If your product is good, a monopoly.*
*But how in the hell d'you expect to sell*
*If you don't do publicity properly!*

Anon

Chapter 12 tries to do three things:

1. To stress the crucial importance of your *curriculum vitae* (CV).
2. To explain how to construct and tailor an immaculate CV.
3. To suggest ways of handling difficult CV questions.

## WHY ADVERTISE YOURSELF?

*Advertisements for Myself* is the title of a revealing autobiography by Norman Mailer, one of America's most pugnacious post-war writers. His title is both characteristic and self-explanatory. It may be considered poor taste to go around blowing your own trumpet. Yet we inhabit a western, capitalist, materialistic world, obsessionally preoccupied with producing and consuming, advertising and selling. Therefore, if you're seeking paid employment—in competition with countless other well-qualified candidates—you must be ready to proclaim your qualities from the housetops. In fact, *you must be ready and willing to sell yourself as many as three times* over to a single potential employer:

- *First*, on paper, in the form of a written letter of application plus your CV.

- *Second*, where required, by submitting yourself to some written intelligence and/or psychological test procedures.

- *Third*, in person, if your written application and test results are good enough to secure you a first (and possibly a final) interview.

Whatever your chosen field of employment, your career specialism or the paid employment you are currently seeking, you will almost invariably have to submit a written application and a CV in response to the job advertisement. Since most college graduates go on to change their jobs several times during the course of a working lifetime, you'd be well advised to maintain an up-to-date CV throughout your subsequent career.

**What is a CV? How should you set about preparing an effective CV? What part does it play in the total recruitment and selection process? What pitfalls should be avoided?**
In earlier centuries, when an ambitious young man (much more rarely a young woman) wanted an appointment at court, or the opportunity to rise in the ranks of the army, commerce or industry, he would often bring a letter of recommendation from some well-connected person, stating that he came of a good family, that his father or grandfather had 'done the state some service', that he showed some talent or promise and that he was therefore worthy of consideration. Or he might provide his own statement of his accomplishments in the arts or science or whatever his chosen field. The best-known of such statements is an undated letter, probably written in 1481, by the youthful Leonardo da Vinci to Ludovico Sforza, Prince of Milan:

Most Illustrious Lord:

Having now sufficiently considered specimens of all those who proclaim themselves skilled contrivers of instruments of war, and that the invention and operation of the said instruments are nothing different from those in common use.

I shall endeavour, without prejudice to any one else, to explain myself to your Excellency, showing your Lordship my secrets, and then offering them to your best pleasure and approbation to work with effect at opportune moments on all those things which, in past, shall be briefly noted below:

1. I have a sort of extremely light and strong bridges (*sic*), adapted to be most easily carried, and with them you may pursue, and at any time flee from the enemy; and others, secure and indestructible by fire and battle, easy and convenient to lift and place. Also methods of burning and destroying those of the enemy.

2. I know how, when a place is besieged, to take the water out of the trenches, and make endless variety of bridges, and covered ways and ladders and other machines pertaining to such expeditions.

3. Item. If, by reason of the height of the banks, or the strength of the place and its position, it is impossible, when besieging a place, to avail oneself of the plan of bombardment, I have methods for destroying every rock or other fortress even if it were founded on a rock, etc.

4. Again, I have kinds of mortars; most convenient and easy to carry; and with these I can fling small stones almost resembling a storm; and with the smoke of these cause great terror to the enemy, to his great detriment and confusion.

9. [*Sic*] And if the fight should be at sea I have many kinds of machines most efficient for offence and defence; and vessels which will resist the attack of the larger guns and powder and fumes.

5. Item. I have means by secret and tortuous mines and ways, made without noise, to reach a designated [spot], even if it were needed to pass under a trench or river.

6. Item. I will make covered chariots, safe and unattackable which, entering among the enemy with their artillery, there is no body of men so great but they would break them. And behind these, infantry could follow quite unhurt and without any hindrance.

7. Item. In case of need I will make big guns, mortars, and light ordnance of fine and useful forms, out of the common type.

8. Where the operation of bombardment might fail, I would contrive catapults, mangonels, *trabocchi*, and other machines of marvellous efficacy and not in common use. And in short, according to the variety of cases, I can contrive various and endless means of offence and defence.

10. In time of peace I believe I can give perfect satisfaction and to the equal of any other in architecture and the composition of buildings public and private; and in guiding water from one place to another.

Item. I can carry out sculpture in marble, bronze, or clay, and also I can do in painting whatever may be done, as well as any other, be he who he may.

Again, the bronze horse may be taken in hand, which is to be to the immortal glory and eternal honour of the prince your father of happy memory and of the illustrious house of Sforza. And if any of the above-named things seem to anyone to be impossible or not feasible, I am most ready to make the experiment in your park, or in whatever place may please your Excellency—to whom I commend myself with the utmost humility, etc.

**Leonardo da Vinci**

## CV STRUCTURE AND FORMAT

The modern CV serves roughly the same purpose. It is a short biographical summary, in which the candidate for some position of paid employment sets out his/her relevant qualifications and experience for the post. The Latin words *curriculum vitae* are used throughout the literate world to convey the meaning 'a summary account of the life of' —so every CV must always be headed with the applicant's full name.

In simple terms, a CV encapsulates scenes from the life of the CV writer. But it's *not* an autobiography, not the whole story. It's important to emphasize that at the outset. Far too many CVs fail to convince because their writers try to say too much. Like the classic skirt-length, a CV should be short enough to be interesting but long enough to be decent. The younger you are, the less you've done with your life, the shorter your CV can be. As you approach adult maturity— say, around your fortieth birthday—your CV must be selective if you're to do justice to significant achievements. By the time you reach 55 (when you'll rarely need a CV!), you'll probably have learned to be ruthlessly selective in what you wish to reveal about yourself.

Before coming to details, we should give some thought to the structure and content of a CV. Here, as elsewhere in life, structure is a function of purpose. In other words, we need to know what purpose a CV serves before we can decide on its most effective structure—one which will help to define its content. Of course, a CV must present factually accurate information (full name, date of birth, address, qualifications, work experience and so on). But a recital of such facts alone is often boring and will rarely secure you that vital interview.

Your CV is, in effect, your visiting card. It gets to your potential employer ahead of you—so it needs to sparkle, to have eye-appeal, to reflect your personality. It need not and should not tell your life story—but it must arouse the employer's interest in you; it must whet his appetite—so that he wants to see you. A well-structured CV serves as an aperitif if it conveys just enough information of the kind needed to secure you that all-important initial interview.

## WHICH FORMAT?

There are three classic formats in which a CV can seek to convey its essential information:

- The *Forward Chronological Format*—which starts logically enough with your name and date of birth and works steadily forwards, telling the story of your life in forward chronological order to the present date.

- The *Reverse Chronological Format*—which starts with a different but equally valid logic from your present position and which unfolds the story backwards, rather like a series of film flashbacks.

- The *Functional Format*—which summarizes your major achievements, highlights your current skills and competencies and specifically targets your job application on a particular employer.

Each format has its loyal adherents, on both sides of the Atlantic and in various parts of the world. Each format has its own peculiar advantages and disadvantages. Which format should you use?

○ The *Forward Chronological Format*—the one with which you're probably most familiar—is popular because it's logical, factual and straightforward. Being traditional in format, it is simple to compile, easy to follow and acceptable to most employers. It takes time and patience for the reader to reach your current position—by which time he/she may have become somewhat bored. And it doesn't always bring out your achievements very clearly. *We nevertheless recommend the Forward Chronological Format because of its clarity, its directness and its acceptability.*

○ The *Reverse Chronological Format* begins by drawing an employer's immediate attention to your current position and your most recent achievements. It starts to 'ring bells' at once, by telling the employer where you're at, right now. To be consistent, all the other information you provide needs to be in the same reverse order—which is somewhat artificial. We all know it's not always easy to follow a story or a film told in flashback. The same is true of a CV. And it may fail to bring out your significant achievements. *We do not therefore recommend this format because it often appears as clumsy, contrived, risky and therefore less acceptable.* But this is a highly personal view. This format may nevertheless be useful to mature graduates, especially those who may have had a period(s) of unemployment, who wish to emphasize their present and future rather than their distant past. The older you are, the less relevant and interesting your early work experience becomes.

o The *Functional Format* dramatically condenses your job application by going directly to the heart of the matter: by stating your employment objectives; by selectively highlighting your experience and major work achievements; and by suggesting how that experience can help this employer to solve his problems, and so meet his objectives. Because it has to be so highly selective, the Functional Format risks the omission of important information which the employer might nevertheless have wished to know about. *This format is nevertheless strongly recommended for certain types of job application.*

## CV *versus* RESUME: IS A MID-ATLANTIC COMPROMISE POSSIBLE?

Over the past two decades, under the pervasive influence of multi-national corporations and the coming of age of the European Community, there have been a number of marked changes in the format and content of what constitutes an acceptable CV in Britain and Europe generally.

The *'Classic British CV'* is characteristically conservative. It favours the *Forward Chronological Format* because it is commonsensical, easy to compile, uncomplicated to read and therefore most acceptable to the majority of potential British employers. The more traditional the industry, the longer established the organization, the more acceptable the Classic British CV. Younger firms in more newly-established industries have a greater tolerance for non-traditional CVs. Most job vacancies advertised in continental Europe call for a manuscript letter of application, a full CV and a recent photograph (but see examples below).

The 'North American Resumé' (accent on last syllable) is an increasingly acceptable alternative to the Classic British CV. As its name implies, it is a further condensation or summarization of the much fuller-length CV, sometimes known in North America by the single-word abbreviation 'Vita'. The *North American-style CV or Vita* is a comprehensive biographical statement, very similar to the Classic British CV, which may run to four or more double-spaced typed pages. A *Resumé* by contrast rarely exceeds one page and is the document most often called for by most American job advertisements in the first instance.

The 'Targetted CV' represents a generally acceptable mid-Atlantic compromise between the full-length 'Classic British CV' and the much shorter 'North American Resumé'. It seeks to combine the essential biographical information found in the former with the closely targetted focus of the latter. It follows the Functional Format described above but includes more details of the kind mentioned above. It seeks to achieve the brevity of the Resumé without sacrificing the all-important achievements required by the Functional Format CV (see example below).

It may be reassuring to learn that CV writers all the world over seem to face very similar problems, as the following poem from Eastern Europe shows:

PREPARING A *CURRICULUM VITAE*


What is required?
Fill out the application
and attach a curriculum vitae.

Regardless of life's length
its outline should be short.

Mandatory are conciseness and selectivity.
Substitution of addresses for landscapes
and firm dates for shaky memories.

Of all the loves only the marital will do
and of all the children only those actually born.
More important than whom you know is who knows you.

Mention travel only if abroad.
Membership in what but without the whatfors.
Honours but without the wherefors.

Write as though you have never talked with yourself
and have always steered clear of yourself.

Say nothing about your dogs, cats and birds,
your precious keepsakes, friends and dreams.

Rather the price than the value, the title than the contents.
Rather the size of the shoes than where he is going,
the person they take you for.

Attach a snapshot too, with one ear exposed.
What counts is its shape, nor what it hears.
And what does it hear?
The clatter of machines turning paper into pulp.

*Wislawa Szymborska*[1]


## QUESTIONS POSED BY CV WRITERS

There are three familiar questions which are asked most frequently by
CV writers:

- *How long should a good CV be?* Since the purpose of a CV is to
  make the most favourable immediate impression on a potential
  employer, the answer must be: the shorter the better, consistent with
  doing justice to the essential content. The ideal length of a CV will
  vary with the age and experience of the applicant and the nature of
  the job vacancy. But one or two double-spaced typed pages will
  generally suffice (see examples below).

- *How do I find room for all the details and still keep my CV reasonably
  short?* An effective CV will convey a judicious selection of essential

[1] The author was born in Kornik, near Poznan, in 1923. She is one of Poland's best-liked
and most-read post-war poets. The translation is by Magnus J. Krynski and Robert
A. Maguire, taken from *Sounds, Feelings, Thoughts: Seventy Poems by Wislawa
Szymborska*, the Lockert Library of Poetry in Translation, Princeton, NJ: Princeton
University Press (1981).

information about the applicant which is most relevant to the particular job application. Since there is no such thing as an 'all-purpose CV', there is no need to include 'all the details'. Your guiding principle should be this: *If in doubt, leave it out.*

- *How much can I decently leave out or gloss over in a CV and still get away with?* This is a tricky question. The guiding principle here is to tell the truth—though not necessarily the whole truth. If, for example, you have a short gap in the chronology of your CV, because you were unemployed or changed jobs several times within a relatively short period—say, six months—you're perfectly justified in omitting all reference to that period by adjusting dates accordingly. Similarly if you were unfortunate enough to be a hospital in-patient or 'detained during Her Majesty's pleasure' for a similar period, you may again choose to omit details. All such omissions, however, must be deliberate and justifiable—not accidental. If challenged, you must be prepared to tell the truth and openly explain your omission.

## STYLE, LAY-OUT AND PRESENTATION

Your CV should *never* be submitted in manuscript form but should always be typed or, better still, word processed/printed and photocopied. There are three important reasons for offering this advice:

1. *Your CV must be legible and never give readers difficulty.*
2. *The employer may wish to photocopy your CV.*
3. *You will wish to tailor and edit your CV for different job applications—therefore word processing is the best idea.*

There is no one best lay-out, type style or print pitch for a CV. Choose a style which reflects your personality; but avoid fussy or 'artistic' lay-outs. Go for simplicity, clarity and eye-appeal. Avoid technical jargon and prefer plain English words to American-English or journalese. Wherever possible, use action-words to convey achievements (see CV examples below). Present information in easy-to-read columns. Allow generous margins for notes. Make sure the sheets are neatly stapled together—and in the correct order. Try not to pepper your CV with punctuation marks (e.g. periods/full stops). A CV is a *curriculum*—a summary—so you don't need to write complete grammatical sentences.

*It is most important that you check, double-check and then recheck your CV for completeness and accuracy. Better still, get someone else to check it independently with you. Nothing is more calculated to reduce your credibility as a serious candidate than blatant spelling or typing errors in your CV. Make sure it's right!*

## RECOMMENDED CONTENT OF A 'CLASSIC BRITISH CV'

| ITEM | POINTS TO NOTE |
|------|----------------|
| **1.** FULL NAME: | Married women should include maiden name (e.g. Mrs Hope Eternal SPRINGS née ETERNAL) |
| | Make clear which is Family Name (e.g. Henry SIMON versus Simon HENRY) |
| | Show gender if not otherwise obvious (e.g. Is Dr Ronnie SMITH male or female?) |
| **2.** DATE OF BIRTH: | Note important differences in international conventions: |
| | In GB, format is Date/Month/Year (e.g. 10/4/70 means 10th April 1970) |
| | In US, format is Month/Date/Year (e.g. 10/4/70 means 4th October 1970) |
| **3.** PLACE OF BIRTH: | Very important for those seeking to work abroad where a work permit may be needed |
| **4.** NATIONALITY: | British or English? Or Irish, Welsh or Scots? |
| **5.** PERMANENT ADDRESS: | Must be in full, with postal code Include telephone number, if appropriate |
| **6.** TEMPORARY ADDRESS: | Only if different from (5) above |
| **7.** PHONE NUMBER: | Consider carefully whether to supply work number as well as home number |

| 8. | MARITAL STATUS: | There are only five categories: |
|----|----------------|--------------------------------|

8. **MARITAL STATUS:** There are only five categories:
   (i) Single
   (ii) Married
   (iii) Divorced
   (iv) Separated
   (v) Widow/Widower

9. **FAMILY CIRCUMSTANCES:** Only if you choose to disclose them!
   Not essential unless relevant:
   (e.g. Child Care Officer; Clergyman, etc.)

10. **EDUCATION:** Best qualification first or last?
    The older you are, the less school certificates matter

11. **EMPLOYMENT RECORD:** Forward Chronology?
    Reverse Chronology?
    NB: Dates must run continuously
    Should show Job Title
    Name of organization
    Main responsibilities
    Major achievements (quantified wherever possible)
    Don't state reason for leaving
    Don't volunteer last salary
    Don't indicate salary required

12. **OTHER INFORMATION:** Membership of Professional Bodies
    Publications, if any
    Extra-mural activities, e.g. Student Union/Society membership
    Offices held, if any
    Sporting or other achievements
    Foreign languages
    (e.g. French—fluent reading/writing;
    Spanish—reading only)

13. **NON-WORK INTERESTS:** Sports and social interests

    **WHAT ELSE?** Don't enclose photograph (unless specifically asked for)

Don't send references (unless specifically asked for)
Don't give hostages to fortune (e.g. by disclosing sensitive information)

## ANNOTATED EXAMPLE OF POORLY-STRUCTURED 'CLASSIC BRITISH CV'

| *Curriculum Vitae* | | | Notes |
|---|---|---|---|
| Name | James G.M. Smith  (**A**) | | (**A**)  Should give all names in full |
| Born | 10/4/60  (**B**) | | (**B**)  Place of birth needed |
| Address | 15 Glenrothes Gardens London NW3  (**C**) | | (**C**)  Is this his permanent address? |
| | (**D**) | | (**D**)  No full postal code? |
| | (**E**) | | (**E**)  No telephone number? |
| Education | 1971–78 | Hampstead Secondary School London NW3 'A' levels—2 'A's and 1 B  (**F**) | (**F**)  Subjects should be given |
| | 1978–81 | BA Camford University  (**G**) | (**G**)  Subjects and class of degree should be given where appropriate |
| Experience | 1983–88 | Ford Motor Company Finance Department  (**H**) | (**H**)  Full job title should be given |

| | | | |
|---|---|---|---|
| **(I)** 1988– | Nissan Motor Company Financial Planning Manager | **(I)** Better to give month and year |
| Other qualifications | French and Spanish **(J)** | **(J)** Degree of fluency should be given |
| Non-work interests | Windsurfing Social Democratic Party **(K)** | **(K)** No hostage should be given to fortune |

## EXAMPLE OF WELL-STRUCTURED 'CLASSIC BRITISH CV'

*Curriculum Vitae* of James G.M. SMITH

1. Full name:           James Garnett McDonald SMITH

2. Date of birth:       10 April 1960

3. Place of birth:      London, England

4. Nationality:         British

5. Permanent address:    15 Glenrothes Gardens
                                 Belsize Park
                                 London NW3 9HJ
                                 (01–456–7890)

6. Temporary address: (until end of June)    Flat 8
                                 Student Hall of Residence
                                 University of Camford
                                 Templeton Street
                                 Camford
                                 Wessex CA3 7KZ
                                 (No telephone number)

7. Marital status:        Married (1984)
                                 Helen Marianne HODSON

| 8. Family: | Peter James McDonald SMITH |
|---|---|
| | (Born 1986) |

9. Education:

| 1971–1978 | Hampstead Secondary School |
|---|---|
| | London NW3 |
| | GCE 'A' Levels in: |
| | French (Grade B) |
| | Economics (Grade A) |
| | History (Grade A) |

| 1979–1981 | University of Camford |
|---|---|
| | B.A. Honours Degree |
| | Class 2 (1) Economics |

10. Employment:

| 1981–1983 | Graduate Trainee |
|---|---|
| 1983–1988 | Financial Analyst |
| | Ford Motor Company Ltd |
| | Central Office |
| | Warley Essex |

| May 1988 | Financial Planning Manager |
|---|---|
| – date | Nissan Limited |
| | Washington Co. Durham |

11. Other information:

Fluent French
Basic Spanish
Computer literate
Car owner

12. Non-work interests:

Windsurfing
Tennis
Play guitar
Hill walking

---

## EXAMPLE OF POORLY-STRUCTURED 'NORTH AMERICAN RESUME'

Monica A Thomas
18 Nautical Lane
► Gloucester, Mass.

Age: 21
Height: 5'6"
Weight: 123 lbs

Hair: Red
Eyes: Hazel
Marital Status: Single

OBJECTIVE

To apply management experience and French language skills in a corporation overseas

EDUCATION

B.A. Management, Georgia State University, Atlanta, Georgia

Also completed a semester of study abroad in London, England (Georgia State University)

ADDITIONAL AREAS OF ACADEMIC COMPETENCE

8 Credit Hours in computers using FORTRAN, Small Business Counselling

College Courses included Marketing, French, English Literature, Computer Programming, Data Processing, Statistics, Sociology, Economics

High School Diploma: St Agatha's High School
Gloucester, Mass: College Preparatory,
National Honour Society
Graduated in top 25% of class

WORK EXPERIENCE

5/83–present

Flowers by Joann, Rockport, Mass
Responsibilities included: bookkeeping, inventory, floral design, selling merchandise, both person to person and by use of computer

5/86–8/86

Waitress, Citronella's Tavern, London, England.
Learned to work effectively with an international clientele.

5/85–9/85

Hostess, The Clam Shell, Salem, Mass.

ACTIVITIES

American Marketing Association
Student Marketing Association,
Fencing Club.

## ANNOTATED EXAMPLE OF WELL-STRUCTURED 'NORTH AMERICAN RESUME'*

| RESUME | NOTES |
|---|---|

RESUME

Monica A THOMAS
18 Nautical Lane
Gloucester, Mass.
01930
(617) 281–0000 **(1)**

**(1)** Phone number essential

OBJECTIVE

To apply management experience and French language skills in a corporation overseas **(2)**

**(2)** Job objective targets work direction

EDUCATION

1987 — BA Management, Georgia State University

1986 — Semester, GSU-London, England

1985–86 — 8 Credit Hours, FORTRAN/Small Business Training Computer Science **(3)**

**(3)** High school eliminated. Didn't enhance

EXPERIENCE

5/83–present (summers) — Flowers by Joann, Rockport, Mass Sales Assistant

**(4)** Sold floral arrangements at $800 to $1200 volume per month **(5)**, in person and by telephone and computer. Managed all details of

**(4)** Use action words
**(5)** Numbers impress reader

144

| | | operation including bookkeeping, inventory and floral design | |
|---|---|---|---|
| 1986 (Summer) | (6) | Citronella's Tavern, London, England Waitress | (6) Writing the year, not just months and year is more substantive |
| | | Learned to work effectively with an international clientele. Cited by manager for outstanding efficiency and courtesy (7) | (7) Any awards or honours should be cited |
| 1985 (Summer) | | The Clam Shell, Salem, Mass. Hostess | |
| | | Established a mood of welcome and enthusiasm | |
| | | Overall patronage increased 35% from June 1 to August 31 (8) | (8) More actual details of real results |
| | | Successfully managed 6 waitresses and 3 busboys (9) | (9) OK to claim credit |
| ACTIVITIES | | Student Marketing Association | |

\* Extracted from The Plymouth Guide to Building a Resumé, *Business Week: Careers*, April/May 1988

## SUGGESTIONS FOR FURTHER READING

CRAC, *Graduate Employment and Training*, Cambridge: Hobsons Publishing (annually).

GO, *Graduate Opportunities*, London: Newpoint Publishing (annually).

# The interview game: Playing to win

*It is better to know some of the questions than all of the answers.*

James Thurber (1894–1961)

Chapter 13 tries to do three things:

1. To explain the crucial importance of the employment interview.
2. To review various forms of employment interview.
3. To suggest how to improve your interview technique.

## EMPLOYMENT INTERVIEWS AND PSYCHOLOGICAL TESTING

In an important 1989 report, the prestigious Institute of Manpower Studies revealed that most UK employers continue to make use of selection methods which are unreliable, unscientific and subject to bias. Many employers pay more attention to body language, dress sense and handwriting than to any real skills and experience. Job hunters, note well!

According to the Institute, a staggering 99% of employers retain their faith in the selection interview in the belief that it is still the most reliable technique. This, in spite of an impressive marshalling of hard statistical evidence—and a growing awareness amongst human resource managers—that the interview lacks overall reliability as an accurate predictor of subsequent organizational performance.[1]

The Institute found that the three most commonly used techniques—interviews, references and application forms—were the three least reliable measures of future job performance. The majority of employers continue to choose a selection method which is cheap and easy to administer rather than one which is reliable but more time-consuming.

As a job hunter, you should nevertheless be aware that, when invited to interview, you may also find yourself invited to take part in one or more *psychological tests*. These tests—consistently shown to be the most reliable method of selection—are used by a mere 16% of employers. They are explicitly designed to reveal dimensions of the candidate's personality which may not always emerge at interview. They therefore serve as a valuable supplementary source of information. Indeed, employers who use such tests now place considerable reliance on the information so derived when making their appointment decisions.

At your next employment interview, you may be invited to undertake one or more psychometric tests—designed to produce some form of psychological profile of the candidate, revealing both strengths and limitations. These psychometric tests should hold no inherent terrors for graduates or professionals. The worst part about them is probably their name—since they imply some dehumanized measurement of the elusive human psyche—and because their results are sometimes poorly interpreted by amateur psychologists.

You should nevertheless be prepared to undertake any psychological tests that come your way—especially when applying for posts which

[1] *Employee Selection in the UK*, London: Institute of Manpower Studies (1989). See also Chris Lewis: 'What's new in selection?', *Personnel Management*, January 1984, pp. 14–16.

you're not certain you want anyway. *In short, take advantage of every opportunity to gain first-hand experience of such tests so that you are not thrown by similar tests for the job which you really do want.*

One frequently used test is *The Kostik Perception and Performance Inventory.* Named after its designer, an American industrial psychologist, the Kostik Test presents you with a set of up to 100 pairs of written statements about various aspects of employment life. You'll then be invited, under some time constraint, to sit down and select one statement from each pair, depending on whichever you think more appropriate to the work situation. For example:

○ *Statement 1*: It's important to get on well with your work colleagues, so that the job gets done.

○ *Statement 2*: It's important to get the job done, regardless of how well you get on with your work colleagues.

In this particular example, you're evidently being invited to say whether you place greater priority on your working relationships or on the job itself. The answer you give to this single forced-choice question is probably less important than any fundamental inconsistencies you may reveal about yourself in your responses to the complete series of such statements.

In a verbal variation on Kostik, you may again be asked to choose between such pairs of statements—this time, speaking your reactions into a portable tape machine, rather than writing down your responses. The results are interpreted in much the same way.

Another form of popular group testing, developing during wartime selection of potential officers and later adapted for use by the Civil Service in selecting administrative officers, involves the use of *simulation exercises*. Here, a group of candidates is brought together and asked to play certain roles in a fictitious organization or to act out their responses to a series of imaginary situations. In this type of exercise, you'll find you're expected to assimilate a good deal of factual information and to display leadership, cool judgement and active team membership as a test of your likely future organizational performance.

In *projection tests*, a subtler and more profound form of psychological probing takes place. You are normally asked to sit in a semi-darkened room and watch the screen as a set of carefully prepared slides are projected for up to five seconds each. When the lights go on after each slide, you'll be asked to quickly write down your spontaneous reactions to the image just projected onto the screen. There's little time for mature reflection and none at all for pretence. What should emerge are your spontaneous, unrehearsed and uncensored reactions to a set of potent visual images—reactions which can be highly revealing of your inner thoughts and feelings to a trained psychologist.

We stress 'to a trained psychologist' because many employers still dabble in fashionable, psychological testing whose value is highly questionable. In the words of two leading academic psychologists:

> The literature on how to make effective selection decisions is large, informative and full of sound advice. Nonetheless, it would seem that organizations more often than not achieve the worst of all worlds in a pretence to scientific precision using techniques that yield 'measures' of doubtful validity, unknown reliability, and untested relevance to them or their candidates' needs.[1]

In view of the growing importance of team working, good communications and inter-personal skills, some organizations are now asking candidates to come to interview prepared to make a *short oral presentation* to the interviewing panel (say, for ten minutes on a topic of your own choosing) and then to answer questions.

*Please remember, however, that all these techniques are supplementary to, and not a substitute for, the classic employment interview.*

## THE ROLE OF THE EMPLOYMENT INTERVIEW

Job hunters sometimes admit they're baffled by employment interviews. How can you do yourself justice, they ask, in such an artificial situation? In any case, what are the selectors looking for? How can you improve your interview technique?

You may find it helpful to think of the employment interview as a ritualistic activity—one of the many fascinating 'games people play' in the advanced industrial societies. To describe it as a game or contest does not detract from the crucial importance of the employment interview or equate it with such trivial pursuits as ping-pong or golf. Rather, it implies that the interview may best be understood as a complex, rule-bound activity in which two or more 'players' are invited to execute a series of more-or-less predictable 'moves' so that the judges can arrive at their decision as to who has won. It is nevertheless a serious game—one in which not all the players can 'win'. As in some other games, there may be no outright winner. Nevertheless, all

[1] Nigel Nicholson and Michael A. West: *Managerial job change: men and women in transition*, Cambridge: Cambridge University Press (1988) p. 157.

job hunters need to master the 'rules of the interview game'—and then to get as much practice as possible if they hope to become an eventual winner.

## A CONVERSATION WITH A PURPOSE

The employment interview might be accurately described as *a private conversation with a public purpose*—the purpose being to enable the selectors to assess the strengths and limitations of various candidates, so as to reduce their number and eventually arrive at the one candidate who represents the 'best fit' with the Job Spec and the Person Spec for the advertised vacancy.

As explained in Chapter 9, progressive employers do not waste their own valuable time—and that of applicants—by inviting candidates to interview who are not qualified *prima facie* for the vacancy they seek to fill. The completed application form, the written letter of application plus the CV or Resumé all represent useful but insufficient sources of information about a candidate's suitability for the job. Why should that be so?

- *First*, because written questions of the open-ended variety permit an unscrupulous candidate to supply what appears to be the 'right answer' and so gain a tactical advantage over a more honest candidate who tells the unvarnished truth about him/herself.

- *Second*, there are certain dimensions of the Job Spec or Person Spec— like character or personality—which are not easily or best judged from the paper evidence alone and which make it highly desirable, if not essential, for the selectors to meet candidates face-to-face.

- *Third*, it must never be forgotten that the selection procedure is always a two-way process. Whilst the selectors are exercising their judgement about the competing candidates, the candidates are equally judging the organization, thereby enabling them to decide whether they would wish to accept an offer of employment if one were to be forthcoming.

## DIFFERENT FORMS OF EMPLOYMENT INTERVIEW

As briefly outlined in Chapter 9, primary and secondary screening of written applications comprise the first two stages of a winnowing process intended to sift or separate out the more attractive wheaten candidates from their accompanying chaff. This 12 stage winnowing process eventually produces a Short List of candidates to be invited to interview. What form is this next stage in the winnowing process likely to take?

An employment interview may take one of several forms:

- *The one-to-one interview*—often favoured by smaller organizations and/or by the senior executive responsible for the final stage of the selection process.

- *The panel interview*—almost universally favoured by most large private sector organizations and an essential feature of public sector appointments where the Selectors are politically accountable for their decisions.

- *The sequenced or tiered interview* comprises a series of one-to-one interviews with different members of the organization in turn. The idea here is to gather impressions of the candidate from several different, well-contrasted managers without having to bring them all together for a panel interview. Candidates are normally screened by more junior managers at lower levels of the organization before being rejected or passed on for further vetting by more senior managers at higher levels of the organization.

- *The democratic interview*, where members of the team in which the successful candidate will work are invited to meet candidates informally to judge their suitability and acceptability within the team and to advise the Selectors accordingly. This type of interview, much favoured for academic appointments in universities and some polytechnics, ought, in theory at least, to be less intimidating because it comprises a relaxed meeting with several of one's future colleagues.

We propose to concentrate here on the first two forms of employment interview—those likely to be encountered by most job hunters—namely, *the one-to-one* and *the panel interviews*—and consider what purposes are served by each.

## THE ONE-TO-ONE INTERVIEW

If the interview is defined as 'a conversation with a purpose'—then the one-to-one interview has one major advantage over the panel interview—namely, that it comes closest to being a genuine conversation with a two-way exchange of information and feelings. By helping to reduce the 'psychological distance' between Selector and candidate, the one-to-one interview should encourage the candidate to relax and talk more freely and candidly. It should therefore help to reduce the psychological strain on both sides of the table. The familiar, conversational, one-to-one type of interview may therefore—in theory at least—seem infinitely preferable to the panel interview in which even the most self-assured candidate may feel intimidated, at least initially.

However relaxed you are made to feel, be on your guard against one major deceptive assumption. *The employment interview is most certainly not a conversation between equals.* A pathetic fallacy, indeed! The employer's representatives are unquestionably the power-holders in this situation whilst you—the candidate—are the supplicant—notwithstanding anything you may have heard recently about employers frantically competing for the services of the so-called best candidates. Of course, there is a measure of reciprocity between the employer who needs to recruit staff and the potential employee who badly needs a job. But their relative needs or desperation are not equal. *The onus or burden of proof is therefore on you* to convince the employer that you need the job, want the job and are better-qualified for the job than any other candidate.

The problem is, of course, that whilst designed to facilitate a better exchange of information and feelings, the *one-to-one interview* is wholly dependent on the 'personal chemistry' between Selector and candidate. Objectively, you may be the 'best' candidate but Selectors don't always arrive at their decisions objectively. In truth, there is plenty of evidence to show that they back their instinctual promptings and are highly subjective in their judgements. Ironically, whilst *the panel interview* may initially appear more intimidating, it does offer the candidate the theoretical possibility of a more balanced set of judgements on his/her suitability for the job.

## THE PANEL INTERVIEW

*The panel interview* is still the most popular form of interview because all those with a strong organizational interest in the appointment can be represented at one and the same time to see that justice is done and hopefully arrive at a faster and more efficient consensus decision on the 'best' candidate. A selection panel may vary in size from three to as many as a dozen Selectors, some of whom will be present in some representative capacity—e.g. trade unions, consumers, etc.

To reduce the risk of any deliberate bias or unlawful discrimination, Selectors do not normally begin to compare their individual assessment of candidates or discuss their relative merits until the last candidate has been seen. The choice of most suitable candidate should then emerge from an impartial consideration of the merits and limitations of each candidate through a process of open discussion.

How is that suitability to be decided? Before they embark on their first interview, wise Selectors will remind themselves of *three key interview objectives* which will assist their subsequent decision-making:

- *First*—to elicit additional information about the candidates to supplement that already obtained from written sources, such as the application form and CV.

- *Second*—to provide candidates with additional information about the job and the organization to supplement that already given in the Job Spec.

- *Third*—to demonstrate a degree of 'fair play' in the conduct of interviews and so convey to candidates as good an impression as possible of the organization. This helps to ensure that the preferred candidate will wish to accept any offer of employment which is later forthcoming. And, even more important perhaps, it leaves the unsuccessful candidates feeling less badly about their rejection.

## WHAT QUESTIONS ARE YOU LIKELY TO BE ASKED?

If the Selectors are to achieve their key interview objectives, they must organize themselves to ask each of the candidates a series of questions— usually, though not always, the same questions—which may be shared out amongst panel members by prior arrangement. *These questions and answers form the heart of the interview.* Despite not being able to anticipate *the exact wording of the questions* you might be asked, you must nevertheless prepare yourself in advance as best you can by considering carefully *the type of question* you might be asked and *the type of answer* you propose to give to each type of question.

Put yourself for a moment in the position of an experienced and professional manager. The Personnel Department has invited you to serve as a member of the forthcoming selection panel and sent you photocopies of the relevant paperwork some days before the interviews are due to begin. Having perused the paperwork, you go through a mental checklist and consider what additional information you think you might need to help you decide on the relative merits of each candidate. You then note under three broad headings the particular questions *you* would like to ask the candidates in order to elicit the additional information you feel you will need to allow you to do your job as a Selector:

- 1. *Does the completed application form or CV and accompanying letter give as clear and comprehensive a picture as possible of this candidate?*
Selectors will often invite a candidate to take them through their CV to clarify and amplify the information already outlined. This may lead in turn to a vast range of supplementary questions of the following type:
(i) Why did you choose these particular subjects to study at School or University?
(ii) Why did you decide to make your career in this particular field?
(iii) To what extent did you come under parental pressure or the influence of some charismatic model in your career choice?
(iv) Why do you think your academic qualifications and experience to date make you a suitably-qualified candidate for this job?

- 2. *Is this candidate sufficiently well qualified and experienced to be successful in tackling the vacancy we're trying to fill?*
Selectors will often pose quite detailed questions to test a candidate's knowledge, skills or attitudes towards the technical content of the job vacancy. Such questions might well be of the following type:
(i) How would you go about achieving such-and-such a task?
(ii) What experience do you have in so-and-so?
(iii) What's your view about the proposed new legislation affecting such-and-such?
(iv) How would you deal with a serious case of so-and-so?
(v) Tell me more about your responsibilities for X at Company Y.
(vi) You appear to have been doing very well at Company Y. What made you decide to move on to Company Z?

- 3. *Has the candidate revealed sufficient of his/her personality and character to enable me to judge how quickly he/she would settle down and successfully fit into our existing team of employees?*
Selectors will often pose any one of a series of quite difficult abstract questions in this area to help them discover more about the candidate's character, motivation, sociability, attitudes to work, commitment, reliability, capacity to deal with stress, and so on. Such questions may be of the following type:
(i) I see you were the youngest of three brothers and two sisters. Were

you spoiled at home as the baby of the family?

(ii) I note that you joined the Student Green Party at university and were elected Sabbatical President in your Third Year. Does that mean you're a fanatical environmentalist?

(iii) You say you spent your undergraduate vacations filling shelves in your local supermarket. Did you learn anything about paid employment from that experience or were you just doing it for the money?

(iv) I see you spent two years in Africa with Voluntary Service Overseas before starting your university course. How easy did you find it to settle down to your studies after that?

(v) This sales job you've applied for involves a good deal of unavoidable stress. How good are you at handling work pressures and the stress that builds up at peak selling times?

(vi) You said in answer to a previous question that your spouse is employed as a Deputy Store Manager with Marks & Spencer and therefore liable to be moved around the country on promotion. Whose career takes priority—yours or your spouse's?

## HOW TO IMPROVE YOUR INTERVIEW TECHNIQUE

Having examined the recruitment and selection process from the Selector's perspective, it should now be easier for job hunters to prepare themselves better for interview and to raise their interview performance. Let's summarize some specific steps you can take to improve your own interview performance:

- 1. Remember that *an employment interview is a business meeting.* You should therefore prepare yourself carefully for your interview and go about it in a thoroughly business-like manner.

- 2. *Professional Selectors and intelligent candidates therefore arrive properly briefed with a full set of relevant papers.* In particular, you should have your own copies of your application and CV to hand throughout the interview. Be ready to refer to them or to make a brief note, if necessary, just as you would at any other business meeting.

- 3. *Recruitment and selection is a two-way process.* The Selectors have called you for interview, but they're also expecting you to be knowledgeable and interested in the organization. Do your homework beforehand and have some appropriately intelligent questions to ask the Selectors, when your turn comes. Don't ask merely factual questions. Use your own questions to score additional points in your own favour.

- **4.** Selectors invariably adopt an inquisitorial role at an employment interview. If they're at all professional, they will have prepared their questions carefully in advance for that role. *You must be on your toes and prepared for any type of question which may arise and then be ready with the type of answer you will give.* If you rehearse the style and content of the answers you'll try to give, the words will generally look after themselves. So, don't learn answers off by heart.

- **5.** Since you know you may be asked to take the Selectors through some aspects of your CV, you should *make some notes for yourself for possible use and rehearse in advance the points you'll wish to make.* Be prepared to begin at any point they designate and make sure you sell yourself positively.

- **6.** Selectors can only achieve their key interview objectives by eliminating candidates, thereby reducing the field as much as possible. They are therefore constantly on the lookout for 'contra-indications'— i.e. any problematic evidence which throws doubt on a candidate's suitability for the job. *Avoid giving 'hostages to fortune'*—i.e. volunteering high-risk information or any other evidence which may lead to your being eliminated on grounds of safety. This does not mean you must always tell the whole truth. In the words of Celia Roberts:

  > It is accepted that candidates should be honest about facts but can tailor the truth so as not to give a bad impression.[1]

- **7.** Selectors tend to believe that their ideal candidate will be positive, optimistic but realistic at all times. You should therefore *try to avoid answering questions in any way which might be construed as negative.* If, for example, you're asked to review your career to date, try to build a positive image of your career development rather than lingering on its negative aspects. In the words of the old song: You've got to accentuate the positive, eliminate the negative.

- **8.** *Be on your guard against 'leading questions'*—i.e. questions whose wording invites you to agree with a predetermined response, rather than leaving you free to answer the question in any way you feel appropriate. For example, you may be asked whether you're in favour of employees joining a trade union of their choice. That's a tricky question but it's open-ended enough to allow you to answer it as you

[1] Celia Roberts: *The Interview Game and How It's Played.* London: BBC (1985), p. 90.

wish. But suppose you're asked: 'I take it you're against employees at managerial level joining trade unions?' You might well reply: 'From the way you've posed the question, I don't seem to have much choice! However, I must say that in my experience . . .'

- 9. Keep a close eye on the time. *Don't allow your answers to run away with you.* Better to give a short appetizing answer and then be asked to amplify it rather than a long boring answer which risks wandering off the point.

- 10. Watch your own non-verbal language at interview and learn to observe and interpret as much of the non-verbal interaction as possible. *Maintain good eye contact with your interrogators,* noting from their faces how they react to your replies. If your early replies are not well received, you may wish to modify your style or your emphasis. *Remember that, in the end, you must be true to your own sincere beliefs.*

- 11. Selectors are often bored by the sameness, the lacklustre self-presentation of many candidates who may be otherwise perfectly good on paper but who disappoint at interview. Without actually getting up on the table to dance, *don't conceal your personality at interview.* You don't have to tell jokes to demonstrate your sense of humour! But you have a sparkle to your personality—why not let it shine through!

- 12. *Work positively to get the job.* But be realistic and recognize that you can't win them all. Innoculate yourself against disappointment and you won't be too depressed if you're not selected for the job. Remember, you can't get too much interview practice—and every interview experience can be made to yield valuable lessons for your next interview.

- 13. *Remember,* this is *not* the time to bargain over an assumed employment offer. But it is the right time to enquire tactfully whether the organization might be willing:

  (a) to assist financially in your relocation from a relatively low-cost housing area (e.g. the North of England, Scotland or Wales) to a high-cost area (e.g. London and the South-East)

  (b) to allow you to accept any offer of employment which might be forthcoming but to defer entry to the organization until after you have completed a higher qualification (e.g. a Masters degree or a PhD)

  (c) to meet the cost of an MBA in, say, three years time if your performance proves satisfactory.

- **14.** *Later*, if an offer *is* forthcoming—especially from a major organization which is keen to recruit you—you may seek to negotiate an improved starting salary or even accept a lump sum payment to enable you to join that organization in preference to any other. Such an 'inducement payment' or 'Golden Hello' may be worth up to £5000 to new graduates who have skills that are in short supply (e.g. in the financial sector) and may be offered to help you, for example, to pay off an outstanding student loan or to help you survive your final year at university or college. You might even persuade an exceptional employer to sponsor you to undertake that Master's dissertation or Doctoral thesis.

## RECRUITMENT AND SELECTION:

The 12-Stage Winnowing Process

Stage 1: Authorization of vacancy
Stage 2: Decision on external recruitment
Stage 3: Publication of job advertisement
Stage 4: Receipt of job applications
Stage 5: Primary screening of written applications
Stage 5: Production of 'Long List'
Stage 6: Secondary screening of surviving applications
Stage 7: Production of 'Short List'
Stage 8: Employment Interviews (plus any supplementary testing procedures)
Stage 9: Decision and employment offer to preferred candidate
Stage 10: Negotiation of Contract of Employment
Stage 11: Letter of acceptance
Stage 12: Rejection of other candidates

## SUGGESTIONS FOR FURTHER READING

Desmond Morris, Peter Collett, Peter Marsh and Marie O'Shaughnessy: *Gestures: their origins and distribution*, London: Jonathan Cape (1979).

E. Berne: *What Do You Say After You Say Hello?* London: Corgi Books (1972).

Lee, J. Cronbach: *Essentials of Psychological Testing*, London: Harper & Row (4th edition 1984) Chapter 11: 'Personnel Selection'.

Michael Pearn, R. S. Kandola and R. D. Mottram: *Selection tests and sex bias: the impact of selection testing on the employment opportunities of women and men*, London: HMSO and Equal Opportunities Commission (1987).

Celia Roberts: *The Interview Game and How It's Played*. London: BBC (1985).

P. Herriot 'The Selection Interview' in P. B. Warr (ed) *Psychology at Work*. Harmondsworth: Penguin (3rd edition 1987).

# Negotiating your first contract of employment

*Let us never negotiate out of fear but let us never fear to negotiate.*

John Fitzgerald Kennedy (1917–1963)

Chapter 14 tries to do three things:

1. To explain the contents of a typical employment contract.
2. To urge you to be more critical before signing your first employment contract.
3. To suggest ways to negotiate a better employment contract.

## WHAT'S IN AN EMPLOYMENT CONTRACT?

For days now—come rain, come shine—you've been scanning the roadway each morning, anxiously awaiting the first mail delivery. You've just about given up, when it drops through the letter box with a satisfying little thud. You almost choke on your nutty crunch flakes! Yet here it is—propped proudly against the milk jug—an offer of employment, elegantly laser-printed in bold black type on corporate notepaper, subscribed with a strong, self-confident signature—an offer of employment for the very job you wanted in one of the most prestigious and successful corporations in town. At last, you've made it! Or have you?

Before you can start work or begin to reduce your overdraft, you must sign your acceptance of *the offer of employment*—which is tantamount to signing *a formal, binding and legally enforceable contract of employment*. So, it pays to know what you're about to do!

When you stop to think, none of us in our right mind would dream of buying our first house or flat (purchase price in 1990? Say, £50 000. Resale value in 2000? Let's play safe: *circa* £100 000) without the benefit of a lawyer's advice. Yet we'll blithely scan our first employment offer (Annual emoluments in 1990? Say, £15 000. Value of 10 years earnings? Let's be ultra-conservative: well in excess of £200 000), sign and return the second copy without consulting a lawyer, without turning a single glossy hair of our otherwise well screwed-on heads.

This realization leads the author to proceed with caution, drawing liberally on the writings of his academic colleagues for clear and authoritative guidance through the mazes of the law of employment in this country.[1]

## WHY BE MORE CRITICAL OF YOUR FIRST OFFER OF EMPLOYMENT?

In order for there to be a contract in English law, certain basic requirements must be met. There must be behaviour which can be construed as the making and acceptance of an offer by the parties, and the resulting bargain struck must be supported by a 'consideration', which is the term lawyers use for a price . . .

[1] Employment law in Scotland differs in certain respects from that in England and Wales. It pays to consult a lawyer.

It is sometimes a matter of some difficulty to know precisely when the bargain was made and how the basic rules are to be applied to it. Is the contract made, for example, when the offer of employment is made (typically, at the end of a job interview), or is it concluded only later when the employee receives a formal letter of appointment (which may contain certain conditions additional to or even inconsistent with what was said at the time of the interview)? No simple general answer can be given to this important question, for it will depend on the facts and how the courts interpret the intention of the parties.[2]

Surely, what Brian Napier, Lecturer in Law at Cambridge University, implies here—for those of us with a mere smattering of legal knowledge—is that we ought to take any offer of employment much more seriously than we do at present. No professional musician, pop star or athlete, for example, would dream of signing a contract for services without first consulting their professional advisors (certainly a lawyer and probably an accountant, too). Yet many professional and managerial employees in industry, commerce and the public services happily sign their employment contracts without taking any kind of professional advice. Perhaps the time has come for us to take a lead from such *artistes* as Liza Minelli and John McEnroe, Ian Botham and Luciano Pavarotti?

My apparently facetious point is underlined by Roy Lewis, Professor of Law, University of Southampton, who says:

This contract [of employment] is complemented not ousted by statutory employment protection. Judicial interpretation of statutory concepts such as dismissal, fairness, redundancy, and continuity of employment has often relied on contractual doctrines, which have been refined and developed in the case law, including the extensive litigation arising from the enforcement of statutory rights. But the point here is that *the contract directly regulates the employment relation, especially where the statutory provisions are either not applicable or inadequate* (our emphasis).[3]

In other words, don't assume that recent employment legislation offers you adequate statutory protection from exploitation by an unscrupulous employer. The employment contract continues to represent an authoritative source of the rules which will regulate the relationship you are about to enter into with your future employer. A heavy onus therefore rests on you to ensure that, so far as possible, you get what *you* want from the employment relationship written into the language of the

[2] Brian Napier: 'The Contract of Employment', in *Labour Law in Britain*, edited by Roy Lewis, Oxford: Blackwell (1986).
[3] Roy Lewis (ed.): *Labour Law in Britain*, op. cit., p. 16.

contract. Unless you do so, the employer may seek to exploit, for example, the recondite distinctions between express and implied contract terms:

> Although the parties are free to make the bargain of their choice, in practice many of the key features of their relationship are left undefined, and are settled by the courts through the device of the implied term. Implied terms are, in legal theory, of secondary significance in defining the contract, in the sense that they will not override express terms which state the contrary, nor can they be used as the basis for an interpretation having this effect. In reality, however, it would be hard to overemphasise either the contribution made by such terms in building up the content of the contract, or the flexibility and power this operation gives to the judges whose job it is to construe the contract.[4]

Take, for example, the question of mutual legal obligations. The employment contract creates a legally enforceable relationship, based on reciprocal rights and duties. Either party may therefore exercise his rights—i.e. seek redress in the courts for any alleged breach of contract by the other party failing to carry out any of his duties, whether explicitly stated or merely implied:

> The employee undertakes, in exchange for the payment of remuneration, to obey the lawful and reasonable orders of the employer, and to take reasonable care in the carrying out of his employment duties. There is also a duty of fidelity towards the employer, which is translated into particular obligations not to enter into competition with him during working time, not to divulge or improperly use confidential information acquired in the course of his employment, and within certain limits, to disclose to the employer information harmful to the employer's interests.
> The employer is bound by a duty to take reasonable care for the safety of the employee, to pay wages, and to exercise due respect and consideration in dealings with the employee. The duty of respect may be seen as the counterpart of the employee's duty of fidelity. It is not of recent creation, but it is a duty which, through the operation of the law of unfair dismissal and, in particular, that part of it concerned with 'constructive dismissal' has acquired a much-increased significance in recent years.[5]

Having clarified the general position, let's take a closer look at the offer-of-employment letter. After the usual pleasantries, and identifying the parties by name and address, the letter will normally provide the following minimum amount of important information:

---

[4] Napier: loc. cit., p. 338.
[5] ibid.

- **1.** *The title of the job* which is the subject of the employment offer—normally the same job title as that contained in the job ad, in your letter of application, and as discussed at interview. *Be on your guard, however, against subtle changes in job title which might affect employment benefits and/or status!*

- **2.** *The amount of (basic) gross annual salary* the employer is offering you for doing the named job—normally the same salary as that discussed at interview. But again, *watch out for any implied or hidden qualifying clauses*—such as performance bonus or increments or compulsory deductions from gross pay.

- **3.** *The suggested date of commencement of employment*—which normally takes into account any contractual notice you're obliged to give your current employer.

- **4.** *The place of employment*—normally that shown on the headed notepaper but it may be different if the offer letter emanates from Head Office but the appointment is tenable at some other part of the organization; or where the job involves considerable travel (e.g. sales personnel) in which case it is necessary for the contract to specify where the job is normally based.

- **5.** *The name of some reference document*—which may be a staff handbook or a collective agreement or some other source of employment rules which, in part, may govern the employment relationship.

## HOW TO NEGOTIATE A BETTER STARTING OFFER

What if the offer letter fails to meet your expectations in respect of any one or more of the items listed above? There's rarely a problem about negotiating a different starting date—for example, to accommodate holiday dates already booked. But what scope is there for negotiating better terms and conditions? How might you set about closing the gap between your expectations and the current offer?

Much depends on the nature of the appointment, the type of organization, the observed management style, the perceived opportunity for bargaining, weighed against the risk of starting off the employment relationship on the wrong foot! Nevertheless, you should not underestimate the extent to which many organizations may be willing to improve on their initial offer—to a candidate whom they really want on board—or to engage in creative pre-employment bargaining.

Suppose, for example, the job ad explicitly stated 'Starting salary £15k–£20k plus removal and relocation expenses up to 20% of first year's salary'. And suppose your present job already pays £12k and that both the old and new job are located in the city in which you currently live. If you're then offered a starting salary of, say, £15k— that's an increase of £3k or 25% in gross pay (i.e. before tax and other deductions)—and you don't need to move home! It's tempting to accept the offer. However, after careful consideration, you might well go back and seek to negotiate a better starting salary using the following three arguments, *inter alia*:

- 1. That, in view of the directly relevant experience you'll be bringing to the job, you're rather disappointed to be starting at the very bottom of the advertised salary range.

- 2. That you've already had an Excellent performance rating this year in your present company which means that, even if you don't move, you're probably already in line for a 10% increase—which would bring your existing salary up to £13.2k. And it's certainly not worth changing companies for a mere £1.8k pa increase in gross pay.

- 3. That, since you already live in the city, you will not need to relocate your home—which means that the organization may have a further amount of £3k up its corporate sleeve, already budgetted in the job ad, to secure your acceptance of its employment offer. (Of course, they'll say that's intended as a single, one-off resettlement payment, not a continuing payroll cost. True. In which case, you might suggest that they make that single payment available to enable you to buy a better car, etc.).

If the new organization *really* wants you on board (and that's sometimes a difficult assessment), it will see the force of your reasonable and well-reasoned argument and won't begrudge raising its offer by, say, another £3k (from £15k to £18k, which means a 50% increase in gross pay) in order to secure your acceptance. It's certainly worth a try! Remember, you're most unlikely to get another chance to improve your starting salary or fringe benefits during your first year of employment with the new organization, unless you negotiate a further salary review after, say, six months probation or 12 months with the organization.

So, how should you set about negotiating that desired improvement in the initial employment offer? By way of illustration, two contrasted accounts are given below of attempts to negotiate a better starting salary before commencing employment, one successful, the other not.

### Alex's story

Alex knew instinctively that the interview had gone well: deeply serious yet good-humoured; edgy yet relaxed; wittily cross-informative; mutually stimulating and gratifying — or so he hoped.

He'd wanted the job badly enough to imply rather than proclaim his natural talent for the role. He'd surpassed his personal best by not pulling out all the stops, not going over the top.

He was not desperate for paid employment—but the job just cried out for him. The way cheddar cries out for chutney. He simply relished the prospect of running his own radio show.

Now came the offer letter. All his expectations were met—except for the fee which seemed much too low. What was the going rate? Where were the natural comparators? He knew the Programme Controller was a tough negotiator who'd chosen a figure he thought he could get away with. Alex enjoyed the irony: the cheddar biter bit.

He took counsel with a close friend. Yes, he wanted the job badly enough to do it for the fee offered—indeed, he'd do it for nothing! But he wasn't prepared to accept the proposed fee without a fight. Counsel agreed: the offer needed to be increased to not less than £$x$ per week. Plus expenses.

Alex called the Head of News to express his disappointment. Take it or leave it, came the cool reply. He took it—without too many later regrets.


### Anthony's story

From the moment the phone rang, Anthony was hooked. The competition was 'boarding' next Tuesday. Would he care to be a candidate? It was for a Senior Producer, Current Affairs. Better salary scale. More increments. He'd be able to buy his new flat *and* keep his car.

Different set-up of course. But more responsibility, more status. A better focused job. Two rungs up the ladder. And of course, a bigger organization, so much better prospects. Thanks very much. He'd be delighted to come for interview.

The interview board was disastrous. Or so he thought. He hadn't brought his own script because they'd forgotten to tell him there was to be a voice test. So he'd read that morning's news—and stumbled twice.

The questions were fair enough. But one of his replies had clearly thrown them. Asked what political documentary he'd prepare for transmission next week, he said he felt the organization overestimated the public's appetite for political news. He'd rather present a documentary on Yuppie Flu. This time *they* were hooked.

The offer letter was romantic in tone but classic in content. The starting salary was too low. Having consulted a trusted friend, Anthony acknowledged the offer and politely enquired if there was any scope for flexibility? He was asked to name his figure. When he modestly did so, they almost took his arm off. It still rankles.


## WHAT CAN WE LEARN FROM THESE ILLUSTRATIONS?

o *First*, that you don't always succeed in your attempt to boost the initial offer.

o *Second*, that you always have the option of *not* accepting the terms on offer.

o *Third*, that you must weigh up all the advantages and disadvantages of the offer before deciding whether to accept.

o *Fourth*, that there's a lot to be said for talking the matter through with a trusted friend or counsellor before taking action.

o *Fifth*, that even if you fail to secure an increase in the initial offer, you have at least let your future employer know how you feel about the starting terms and conditions.

o *Sixth*, that nobody is indispensable, so if you don't accept the offer, there's usually somebody else who will.

*Good luck in negotiating your next offer of employment!*

### SUGGESTIONS FOR FURTHER READING

Brian Napier 'The Contract of Employment' in Roy Lewis (ed): *Labour Law in Britain*, Oxford: Blackwell (1986).

Roger W. Rideout: *Principles of Labour Law*, London: Sweet & Maxwell (2nd edition 1976) Chapter 4: 'The Formation of the Contract of Employment'.

# Congratulations on securing your first job!

*Remember at all times that pleasure and grief go together.*
*Keep faith with pleasure and face grief with courage.*

Robert Schumann: *Inscription on flyleaf of his piano*
*volume:* Davidsbündlertänze

Chapter 15 aims to do three things:

1. To congratulate you on securing your first career appointment.
2. To point out some risks and opportunities which now lie ahead.
3. To suggest how you can make the most of your new appointment.

## RISKS AND OPPORTUNITIES IN PAID EMPLOYMENT

Congratulations, indeed! It's a momentous occasion. The fact that thousands of other young people in Britain—and around the world—notch up the same achievement each year should not detract from your own satisfaction and sense of personal achievement. Whatever else you may do in a long and rewarding career, there's no other day quite like the day on which you step into paid employment for the first time ever. What joy! What immediate risks? What career opportunities lie ahead?

As you make your way to work that first morning, your mind reels with excitement. Adrenalin courses through the blood. The opportunities seem boundless. There's no apparent limit to what you may now achieve in your future career. Whether you're content to browse the comfortable middle meadows of your career or ambitious to scale the hungry heights, we wish you every possible success—hoping you will recognize and then take advantage of some of the opportunities that lie ahead!

Of course, you have your contract of employment tucked safely away at home, or stored perhaps at the bank. For no matter how big the organization, your job makes you acutely vulnerable once you start employment. Most employers therefore insure their employees against certain known risks from day one. Though you may have to serve a minimum qualifying period, usually six months, before being admitted to the organization's pension plan, from today you (or rather your estate) may be entitled to the equivalent of one full year's gross salary tax-free in the event of your death in employment. That should make you feel even better!

So, whilst your employer spreads the risk by paying a specially calculated insurance premium, usually based on total payroll, it's up to you to decide whether that cover offers sufficient protection to you and your loved ones, in the unlikely event that anything serious should happen to prevent you from continuing to earn and to build a long and successful career.

Take, for example, the risk that the organization which you've just joined flourishes so successfully under your benign influence that it results in some form of merger or take-over—now so fashionable. Will there still be a reasonable job for you in the newly-merged and enlarged organization? Let's hope so. But you never can tell.

Compare and contrast (as they say in exam questions) your own employment vulnerability with that of your exact counterpart—the typical Japanese graduate setting out on his/her first career appointment.

Japanese society is in many ways more efficient—some would say more ruthless, more materialistic—than our own in the West. Having struggled and successfully overcome the horrendous competitive barriers found in higher education, what you're looking for in your first paid employment in Japan is not merely a good starting salary and interesting, rewarding work to do. You also want to know that you have job security—an abiding feature of the highest priority amongst the educated, managerial classes of Japan. What most Japanese firms therefore offer their top cadres (i.e. technical, professional and managerial staff) is something we translate as 'lifetime employment'— a broad measure of job and income security which may indeed last a lifetime.

Alongside this *system of lifetime employment* which caters for the needs of a permanent, highly-qualified minority, lies the parallel system which covers the vast majority of other, non-permanent Japanese employees—namely, the temporary or continually changing workforce, whose strength fluctuates with the fortunes of the organization, like fluctuations of the tide or the stock market.

The protection offered to Japan's employment elite by lifetime employment does not simply reflect the social conscience of Japanese employers. Rather, it's a splendid example of enlightened self-interest. For, just as the employer invests in new graduates by including them and their families in the organization's total security system, so the graduates represent human capital whose asset value accrues to the employer by virtue of the fact that they mostly bind themselves to that one employer for the rest of their working lives. In return, the organization cherishes the loyalty which lifetime employment inspires and so looks after its graduates even more assiduously. Japanese lifetime employment is thus mutually reinforcing.

Contrast that employment security with the very limited security offered by organizations in the West. Of course, the longer you stay with any one organization, the less likely you are to suddenly leave— or to be axed. Conversely, the highest turnover of technical, professional and managerial talent normally takes place during the first couple of years of employment. You may find, for example, that you don't after all enjoy the work or the organization as much as you thought you would—or that the organization fails to demonstrate its appreciation of your work, as you would wish. Whichever way around, you part company—and start all over again. It happens every day in many British organizations.

What can you do—what should you do—to protect yourself in advance against the more ravaging effects of this ever-present vulnerability? Well, you might begin by posing relevant questions about the organization's pension plan and life assurance package *before* you accept the employment offer. Indeed, it's an excellent idea to ask your future employer for a copy of the relevant Rulebooks covering these matters and to have them vetted by an independent financial adviser.

Whether or not your current employer provides adequate cover for you and your family, you can—and should—give serious consideration to taking out additional private life assurance and making further pension provision. For an appropriate premium payment, you can insure against practically any risk you care to nominate—from the remote possibility that England might win the next Test Match against Australia, to the chances of it being dry and warm in London next Midsummer's Day. If there's a statistical risk, you can insure against it happening to you and yours, at Lloyds of London!

**The following sections are unavoidably technical,[1] so fasten your thinking cap! But don't skip these sections—or you risk losing out financially throughout your future career!**

To most people starting out on their careers, planning for their longer-term future may seem the least of their concerns. But, as many older people have found to their cost, it's never too early to plan for the future. Your own circumstances and financial situation must dictate how you spend your money. But before you consider taking out any life assurance or making any investments, it's worth asking yourself the following questions:

1. *What benefits are offered under my employer's pension plan?*
2. *How far do I want to protect my family (if any)?*
3. *Do I want to commit myself to a regular monthly outlay?*
4. *Is there any long-term aim in mind—buying a car? A house? Saving for a holiday?*
5. *Can I afford to take any risk with investments?*
6. *Do I need immediate access to my money?*

*Pensions schemes* should be considered first because your personal financial planning must depend on whether or not you're adequately covered by an employer's pension scheme and whether or not you

---

[1] Grateful thanks are due to Julian Mounsey of the Clerical and General Investment Group of the Clerical, Medical and General Life Assurance Society for the technical information contained in the following pages. Further information or advice may be obtained from the Society on 0272–290566.

consider the level of benefits provided to be adequate. The three basic options available for any employee are:

○ **1.** *To rely solely on the State pension scheme.*

○ **2.** *To rely on the employer pension scheme plus the State pension scheme.*

○ **3.** *To add personal pension schemes to your employer's pension scheme and the basic State pension scheme.*

For the self-employed, the options are limited to the State basic pension scheme and/or a personal pension plan.

## YOUR STATE PENSION

There are now two elements to the State pension scheme: a flat rate basic pension and the State Earnings Related Pension Scheme (SERPS) which is also known as 'the additional pension'.

### BASIC STATE PENSION

Employees and self-employed paying National Insurance (NI) contributions will normally qualify for the basic pension. The basic pension is generally increased each year in line with inflation and for the year 6 April 1989 to 5 April 1990, it amounted to £43.60 per week for a single person and £69.80 for a married couple.

### THE STATE EARNINGS RELATED PENSION SCHEME (SERPS)

Only employees can qualify for a pension from SERPS. The self-employed cannot build up benefits in this way. The actual calculation of the amount of SERPS pension is complicated and will depend on the earnings in the years in which full rate NI contributions are paid. The maximum SERPS pension for those reaching retirement age after the year 2008 will be 20% of average earnings during their working career between what are known as the Lower and Upper Earnings limit. The Lower Earnings limit is roughly equal to the basic State pension (£43 per week in 1989/90) and the Upper Earnings limit is the maximum earnings on which employee NI contributions are paid (£325 per week in 1989/90). Note that *the **maximum** SERPS pension in today's terms would still only amount to about £55 per week!* But your SERPS pension will increase after retirement in line with inflation.

### OPTING-OUT OF SERPS

It's possible to 'contract out' or 'opt out' of SERPS through a *personal pension plan* or through an *employer's pension scheme*. By contracting out, you give up part of your SERPS and instead receive benefits from the personal pension or employer's scheme. All employees now have this option and it's generally believed that for younger employees (under 45 for men and under 35 for women) *it's beneficial to contract out.*

## EMPLOYERS' PENSION SCHEMES

Many employers provide a pension scheme for their employees and, in the past, it was often compulsory for those eligible to join. Since 1988, however, every employee has the right to leave their employer's scheme or to choose not to join in the first place. Before you decide whether or not to join an employer's scheme, if one is available, it's important to consider the pros and cons of the scheme and to seek advice on alternatives.

An employer's pension scheme will generally provide the following benefits:

o 1. An income in retirement.

o 2. An income for a widow or widower or other dependants on death before or after retirement.

o 3. A lump sum for dependants on death in service.

o 4. On retirement, it is usually possible to take part of the benefits as a tax-free cash sum.

The overall benefits under an employer's pension scheme are limited by rules laid down by the Inland Revenue.

### FINAL SALARY SCHEMES

For those in a 'Final Salary' scheme, the retirement income is based on earnings in the last (few) year(s) before retirement and on the number of years' membership of the scheme. The most common bases are 1/60th or 1/80th of earnings for each year in the scheme.

### MONEY PURCHASE SCHEME

Until recently, the most common basis for an employer's pension scheme was final salary, but it's now more usual for new schemes to be on a 'money purchase' basis. Under a money purchase scheme, the benefits payable are based on the contributions paid by the member and the employer—and the investment growth obtained. Unlike a final salary scheme, no guarantee is given as to the level of pension benefits.

## PERSONAL PENSION SCHEMES

Personal pension schemes are available for the self-employed and to all employees who are not entitled to pension benefits from an employer's scheme. These schemes offer a wide choice of alternative investment options and are available from insurance companies, friendly societies, unit trust companies, banks or building societies.

Personal pension schemes, like employer schemes, receive very advantageous tax reliefs from the Inland Revenue. Contributions qualify for tax relief as do an employer's contributions if he is also prepared to contribute. The funds in which contributions are invested are free from both Income and Capital Gains Taxes, and, as in employer schemes, part of the benefits may be taken as a tax-free cash sum.

All personal pension plans are 'money purchase' schemes. Contributions are built up in a fund until retirement when an annuity is purchased to provide an income for life. The amount of pension at retirement will depend on how well the investment grows. Depending on personal circumstances, it's also possible to provide for a widow or widower.

## WHICH PENSION ROUTE?

It's impossible to give any general answer as to which type of pension scheme is likely to be most beneficial to you. The best scheme for any individual will depend on age, personal circumstances, personal attitudes and, of course, the level of benefits an employer will provide. Some of the considerations are as follows:

- A personal pension offers personal control, confers a wide investment choice, can easily be taken from job to job, and can be tailored to meet your personal needs.

- A company scheme is likely to be less flexible, but to offset this, the employer is likely to contribute more than the employee (in many schemes only the employer contributes). A package of benefits will be offered — in many cases substantial—and very expensive to match. If an employer operates a pension scheme it is generally unlikely that he will be prepared to contribute to a personal pension scheme.

## LIFE ASSURANCE PROTECTION

The primary purpose of life assurance, and its ideal, is to provide dependants with reasonable financial security in the event of a bread-winner's death. Before planning to invest for the future, it's sensible to ensure that you have adequate life cover.

### TERM ASSURANCE

Term assurance is life assurance taken out for a specified period, payouts being made only should death unfortunately occur within that period. A term assurance policy would be used to cover circumstances such as:

o  1. When a house mortgage or other loan is required.

o  2. When an income for dependants may be required.

o  3. When a young family is growing up.

### LEVEL TERM ASSURANCE

This is the simplest form of term assurance with the amount of cover remaining constant throughout the specified period of the policy.

### CONVERTIBLE TERM ASSURANCE

This works in the same way as level term assurance, but is particularly useful if you need substantial life cover at minimal cost, and expect that you will need to review your life assurance at a later date. Options allow you to convert to one of a range of policies, irrespective of your state of health, occupation or place of residence, throughout the term of the original policy.

### DECREASING TERM ASSURANCE

The sum assured is fixed at the outset and reduces each year, either by level amounts or to correspond with the amount outstanding under a repayment mortgage.

## FAMILY INCOME COVER

This will provide a family with a tax-free income on the death of the life assured for as many years as the policy has to run.

## WHOLE LIFE ASSURANCE

Whole life assurance differs from term assurance in that it provides permanent rather than temporary cover, unless premiums are discontinued. As the name implies, cover can continue until the day you die, benefits being payable only on your death. But this is a more expensive means of providing protection than term assurance.

# SAVINGS AND INVESTMENTS

There's a very wide range of alternative savings and investment mediums for you to consider in addition to the traditional building society or bank deposit account or National Savings scheme. The actual choice of investment will depend again on your personal circumstances, your attitude to risk, and whether or not you wish to invest a lump sum or save on a regular monthly or annual basis. What follows is necessarily a brief description of the principal choices available to you.

## WITH-PROFITS ENDOWMENT ASSURANCE POLICIES

Endowment assurances are used mainly to provide a lump sum at a specific date in the future, usually between 10 and 30 years time. You also receive life cover during the term of the policy. Endowment assurances can also be used to repay a house mortgage or other loans. Under a with-profits endowment assurance there is a guaranteed sum payable at the end of a fixed term to which bonuses are added each year. These bonuses are known as 'reversionary bonuses' and once added to a policy are guaranteed. The level of bonuses will depend on how well the insurance company's investments perform. In addition, when benefits are paid there may also be an additional 'terminal' bonus.

The insurance company spreads the risk over a range of investments and good and bad years are usually smoothed out. There is normally no tax on the proceeds unless the policy is called in early, in which case there is a potential liability for higher rate tax if the policy has been in force for less than $7\frac{1}{2}$ years (10 years for longer term policies).

If you're looking for a regular monthly savings plan with a steady return higher than you would receive from a building society, bank or National Savings, then an endowment assurance is well worth considering provided that you want to go on saving for at least 10 years. If you're buying a house, a low cost endowment mortgage is also worth considering.

## UNIT TRUSTS

There's now an ever-growing choice of unit trusts both for lump-sum investment and regular monthly savings. When you invest in a unit trust, your money is pooled with that of other investors to buy a wide range of stocks and shares. Each pool is divided into units and the investor receives a number of units depending on the amount of his/her investment. The price of units fluctuates depending on the performance and value of the underlying investments held by the trust.

The range of unit trusts on offer means that you can select from low-risk to high-risk investments, depending on your own particular requirements and investment philosophy. It's possible to invest in a wide range of UK shares, in overseas stock markets, in specialized sectors or markets, or in fixed interest stock known as 'gilts' (i.e. gilt-edged investments). For the more cautious investor, 'managed funds' investing in a range of other unit trusts are now on offer. There's no minimum period for which you must invest in a unit trust, but when you sell units, the profits you make are subject to Capital Gains Tax, but currently (1989/90) gains up to £5000 are tax free in any year.

## UNIT-LINKED SAVINGS PLANS

A unit-linked savings plan is a regular savings plan which is essentially a unit-linked endowment assurance. Like an endowment assurance, it's necessary to contribute for at least 10 years to receive the full benefits of such a plan and it's also possible to link a plan to mortgage repayment. However, it's more risky than an endowment assurance and there's no guarantee on the return you will receive. In a unit-linked plan, as in a unit trust, premiums are invested in units and the value, when the proceeds are taken, will directly reflect the value of the underlying investments at that time.

It's possible to reduce the risk by selecting a 'managed' fund where there's a spread over a range of investment types. Alternatively, it's possible to invest in funds which are invested on a specialized basis, for example, in UK stocks and shares, overseas, or in gilts or property. You can also switch your money between funds of a particular market which seems more attractive.

## PERSONAL EQUITY PLANS (PEPs)

Personal Equity Plans, commonly known as PEPs, offer a significant advantage in that up to £4800 (in 1989/90) can be invested with no liability for tax on any income or Capital Gains. Up to £2400 per annum of the £4800 allowance can be paid to Unit Trusts, PEP invested in UK shares, or in investment trusts. The remaining amount must be invested directly in UK shares. PEPs have significant tax advantages but are generally a fairly risky form of investment.

## OTHER INVESTMENTS

We've dealt above with the more popular forms of investment which may be most appealing to those who are starting on a career. You may also be attracted to other forms of more specialized investment, such as direct investment in stocks and shares, investment trusts and insurance bonds. *Before entering into any such investment, it's important that you consider very carefully the element of risk involved and obtain independent financial advice where necessary.*

## MAKING THE MOST OF YOUR NEW APPOINTMENT

Let's take an optimistic view and assume that you've made a good decision to accept the offer of employment with this employer, and that you settle down quickly and successfully in your new job. How should you make the most of your appointment?

During your first days and weeks of employment, your mind will undoubtedly be engrossed, consciously or unconsciously, in processing a mass of new data: learning the new organization chart; discovering who's who; putting names to faces and places; finding out about organizational politics. This can be an exhausting business, especially where the charts and the names have not been kept up to date. You'll probably go home mentally exhausted every evening. But this phase doesn't last long.

It's an excellent idea during the first phase to *maintain a simple but effective job log*, capturing your first impressions of the organization. It doesn't have to be a polished literary work—just a series of nightly jottings or recorded thoughts on the day's more significant encounters: whom you met; the impressions they made; what you discussed; significant gleanings about organization policy and its critics; the essential procedures and protocol you're expected to observe; the successes and failures, the risks and opportunities being discussed amongst influential members of the policy-making group. That log will sustain you in the years ahead.

A second point worth making is that, during your early weeks of employment, you can pose almost any deliberately provocative or innocent question you choose—and get away with it! Why do we do things this way? What's the point of this policy? How does that policy help us achieve our stated objectives? How long has this been going on? That kind of question. And note the reactions your question provokes amongst your colleagues!

A third point is to *avoid any possible accusation of intellectual arrogance* (especially on the part of non-graduates) by rushing into judgement where managerial angels fear to tread. Instead, try to exercise restraint, impose a self-denying ordinance, hold back and generally avoid coming forward with helpful, positive, constructive, imaginative solutions to problems which you perceive all around you from day one. Note them all, write down your tentative solutions back at home, keep them in a safe place—but don't dare to come out with them unless invited—or at least until after you've completed one month's employment in that department or office. Be inquisitive, be shrewd, but above all be provident and keep your luminous intelligence under wraps for at least four weeks. You'll have plenty of opportunities to shine in the months and years ahead, provided you don't dazzle them into embarrassment too soon!

A fourth point is to really *get to know your immediate boss*, his/her strengths and limitations and personal idiosyncracies; how well or poorly organized as a manager; how good a communicator; how good a listener; whether responsive to new ideas and suggestions for improving departmental performance; when best approached with new ideas—Mondays or Fridays, mornings or afternoons; public fears and private anxieties; marital status, family background, etc. In short, you need to know how to impress your boss most favourably by timely, relevant, constructive and, above all, acceptable interventions which help him/her to achieve organizational targets and objectives within given resource limitations.

Never forget, it's your immediate boss who compiles the detailed report on your first year's performance. That report goes onto your personal file and so crucially influences how you're perceived by more senior managers in the organization hierarchy. And their perception, in turn, will be largely influential in determining how rapidly you'll be promoted.

## WHAT ABOUT THE DOWNSIDE?

Suppose you find you've made a genuine mistake in your first career appointment. How should you gracefully disengage from uncongenial employment after less than one year of entering the organization? There are few rules and they are simply stated.

- *First*, look before you leap. Otherwise, you may simply be exchanging the frying pan for the fire!

- *Second*, make sure you can justify to yourself taking so great a step as leaving your first employment after so short a period. You may be right to contemplate leaving. Above all, it's you who will principally have to live with the decision to quit. Will that decision come back to haunt you?

- *Third*, ask yourself how you will satisfactorily explain to a third party—e.g. your next potential employer—your twin decisions: (a) to join the organization in the first place, and (b) to leave it after less than one year of joining.

- *Fourth*, if you are considering leaving for reasons other than some form of discrimination or sexual harassment, ask yourself how much better you'll feel about the decision to leave, after completing one full year in the post. There are three reasons for this:

  - (*i*) Although there is nothing magical in a 12-months anniversary, a potential employer might take the view that you'd quit before giving the job a fair trial in less than one full year.

  - (*ii*) On completing 12 months in the post, you're reasonably entitled to ask your boss for a formal review of your work performance and a discussion of levels of satisfaction on both sides.

  - (*iii*) Despite the fact that you've decided to leave before 12 months are up, you may still wish to call on the organization for some form of job reference. You simply compound your problems if you've failed to convince your present employer that you've given the job and the organization a fair trial by leaving without at least completing your first full year of employment.

- *Finally*, before offering your resignation, ask whether you've given yourself every chance to effect that essential double accommodation which goes with every new appointment—first, to adjust yourself to the organization, the job and your new colleagues; and second, to mould your work role to suit your personality and personal needs. Edgar Schein, distinguished organization analyst, describes these frequently-observed adjustments as 'reactive' and 'proactive' coping strategies.[2] Whatever your job, whatever your career, you must make a positive and sustained effort to effect this double adjustment so that, whatever the outcome, you can live with yourself thereafter.

Whatever lies ahead of us in our first career appointment, we may do well to reflect along these lines. In childhood, we're told that schooldays are the happiest days of our lives. We're told to make the most of our college days because they'll never come again. Now, as we launch into our chosen careers, we must surely make the most of *these* years— or what chance do we stand of ever enjoying our far-distant retirement?

### Malcolm's story

When I first met him in Malta in 1949, Malcolm was a junior Naval Stores Officer, fuelling the British fleet. Back in the UK, he'd been a commuting Admiralty clerk. Here, he had an elegant apartment, enjoyed cheap gin, wrote poetry and wore pale lemon gloves.

He'd joined the Civil Service straight from school and professed to loathe the whole inefficient, mismanaged, bureaucratic business. Temperamentally they seemed well suited but he had bold, romantic, if unrealistic, plans for his career.

Malcolm couldn't wait to get back 'home' where he would help to spearhead the great Grimond-led Liberal Revival of the 1950s. He would take leave of absence and stand for Parliament. The Commons was, after all, 'the best club in the world'.

Back home, he was posted congenially to the Hamble Estuary, near Portsmouth, where he continued to lead a seemingly charmed existence, with short commuting, cheap housing and long sailing week-ends. Denied promotion, he lamented his career prospects, lampooned his ineffectual bosses, one of whom, Stainer, was subjected to his daily crucifixion.

Malcolm was unlucky in love as well as in his work. His first wife died tragically and his second, much younger, ran off with his money. For ten years, he insisted on bringing up his own son, who turned into a fine man and a good architect.

Malcolm continued to fret and count the days to retirement. The Liberal Revival faltered, then collapsed. In his 50s he seized the

[2] E. H. Schein: *Career Dynamics: Matching Individual and Organizational Needs*, Reading, MA: Addison-Wesley (1971).

chance to retire early on a miniscule pension. His third marriage seems wonderfully serene—his life at last fulfilled as an assiduous member of the House of Laity of the Church of England.

## SUGGESTIONS FOR READING READING

J. Gordon and P. Wilson: 'What makes people change jobs?', *Personnel Management*, Vol 14, pp 22–25, (1982).

E. W. Richards: 'Undergraduate preparation and early career outcomes: a study of recent college graduates', *Journal of Vocational Behavior*, Vol 24, pp 279–304, (1984).

J. A. Arnold: 'Tales of the unexpected: surprises experienced by graduates in the early months of employment', *British Journal of Counselling*, Vol 13, pp. 308–19, (1985).

C. Mabey: *Graduates into Industry*, London: Gower (1986).

# chapter

# 16

# Training, personal growth and career development

*Between the ages of twenty and forty we are engaged in the process of discovering who we are, which involves learning the difference between accidental limitations which it is our duty to outgrow and the necessary limitations of our nature beyond which we cannot trespass with impunity.*

W. H. Auden (1907–1973): *The Dyer's Hand*

Chapter 16 tries to do three things:

1. To place your further training within a career context.
2. To encourage you to monitor your own personal growth.
3. To help you with your career development.

## MAKE YOUR GARDEN GROW!

A career is much like a garden: a thing of potential beauty and a source of perennial satisfaction—but one which requires cultivation, nutrition and continuous attention, if it's to be fully productive. Left to itself, it soon becomes overgrown, almost beyond redemption. How should you go about ensuring that your career flourishes in the way you would wish?

We begin by drawing a somewhat sharp distinction between two broad groups of graduates—those whose tertiary education included a substantial measure of technical or vocational training—like doctors or dentists, farmers or pharmacists, lawyers or actors, musicians or painters, designers or divines—and those whose degree courses were intended to provide an essentially rigorous intellectual training, with little or no specific vocational content—like those who read Arts or Social Science.

This latter group must pay particular attention to their postgraduate education and development. It's tempting to argue that—since you've managed to avoid any vocational training thus far—you can continue to do so without damaging your future prospects. That's no longer true. In due course, we'll need to consider carefully whether you should now pursue some form of general management qualification (e.g. a Master of Business Administration degree) or, say, a career-specific or even a job-specific qualification (e.g. a Master's degree in Public Administration) or something roughly halfway between the two (e.g. a Diploma in Management Studies in one of several broadly defined specialist subject areas).

If, on the other hand, you went through medical, veterinary or dental school, you know that your future career depends on your ability to extend and deepen your technical knowledge and to practise and hone your vocational skills. There are professionally-defined standards of continuing education and training, with examination or assessment procedures automatically built into your career plan for many years to come. The same holds true for others whose first degree confers partial exemption from the professional or vocational examinations of their respective professional institutions—in accountancy, architecture, aeronautical engineering and so on.

Whichever of these two broad groups you fall into, a discussion of your continuing education and development needs should figure prominently amongst the list of priority subjects dealt with during your induction to the organization you join on accepting your first offer of paid employment. *Induction or initial training* is now a common feature of most progressive organizations. It normally covers a wide range of issues—from organizational history and structure to current policy and procedures, from how you get paid, taxed, insured and cared for, in sickness or in health, to sports and social facilities and much else besides.

In addition to group induction, there will ideally be a separate discussion between you, your boss and/or the manager responsible for administering education and development programmes, which deals specifically with *your personal education and training needs*, based on a mutual appraisal of what's required to bring you up to some minimally acceptable standard of work performance.

It's difficult to be specific across the entire spectrum of general managerial or administrative work but let's consider *computer literacy*, by way of illustration. The microelectronic revolution has profoundly transformed the working lives of employees in almost every occupation—wherever information is stored, retrieved, manipulated, transmitted, received, or acted upon. So, whatever your specialist area of work, sooner or later you'll need hands-on experience in operating a computer, if only as a word processor.

There's no doubt whatever in the mind of this writer, that the lives and careers of graduates in the last decade of this century and beyond will be dominated by the computer just as the lives of most employees were dominated a century ago by the coming of cheap, safe electricity. It is therefore an act of enlightened self-interest to *master the basic QWERTY keyboard skills* as soon as possible and to make yourself computer literate within a realistic target date. Whether you need to go on and master various computer languages, the use of spread-sheets and so on, depends on your vocational choice. Make sure you include such questions in the discussion of your personal training plans when you next meet your line manager and the education and training advisor.

Whether your career then develops along *specialist or generalist* lines depends on a number of factors, including your own personality type (see Chapter 5), the sector, industry and type of organization in which you choose to work, and the career opportunities which present themselves at strategic points in your career development. You may begin within a broad general function (e.g. finance, sales, marketing, personnel); then be invited by your employer to change specializations within that function, as the organization's needs change and develop. You may then decide, as part of your career development plan, to extend your specialist knowledge and experience by changing organizations within the same industry—or by moving into a completely different industry. Later still, you may make a further significant career change, reverting from specialist to generalist, from practitioner to consultant and trainer, depending on changes in personal needs and circumstances and the available career opportunities.

### Sander's story

Sander left school at 18 with four A levels but no career strategy. After National Service in the Royal Navy, he joined the Salaries and Pensions Division of the Ministry of Education. Bored and frustrated by low-grade, undemanding work, he began WEA evening classes and made his way, as a mature student of 25, to the LSE where he graduated in 1956 with a First Class Honours Degree in Economics and Political Science.

At age 28, he joined a major steel corporation as a Personnel Manager specializing in vocational education and training. At age 32, he was invited to move into Industrial Relations and became a specialist in pay structures, job evaluation and collective bargaining in steel.

At age 36, he made a major career shift and joined Ford Motor Company as a strategic planner in Industrial Relations. Over the next nine years, he held various posts of increasing responsibility within personnel, finishing with a wide-ranging remit as Ford's Personnel Services Manager, Central IR Staff.

At age 48, following the second oil shock, Sander took advantage of a voluntary redundancy programme to leave Ford to read for a Masters Degree in Industrial Relations and Personnel Management back at the LSE. There he was later offered a teaching post in Industrial Relations and settled down to enjoy a new and rewarding career as an academic and management consultant.

From 1984 to 1988, Sander was Senior Lecturer and Deputy Head of Industrial Relations at the Strathclyde Business School in Glasgow. He retired early at age 60 to devote more time to his writing, to career consultancy, to management training — and to launching another new career — in commercial radio.

## THE SELF-DISCOVERY WHEEL

Kurt Hahn, a political refugee from Nazi Germany, who settled in Scotland and subsequently founded Gordonstoun School, based his entire educational philosophy and life's work on his mature view that human life is concerned above all with three inseparable personal needs—growth, development and fulfilment. Long after we've ceased growing physically, we continue to grow in intellectual, psychological and spiritual dimensions. And to that extent, we continue to develop our innate capacities and to fulfil our potentiality.

Although the organization for which you work probably operates some form of annual performance appraisal, it's very much your responsibility to ensure that you monitor your own personal growth. That monitoring is not always easy because we rarely take the trouble to invest time and care in taking stock of our own psychological development. What's to be done, then?

If you follow Hahn's general argument—if you're concerned with your own personal growth, development and fulfilment, this is a good time to take stock of your own life and career, through *The Self-Discovery Wheel*.

*The Self-Discovery Wheel aims to help you build a more satisfying and rewarding career.* It provides the opportunity for you to take stock of your life and your career in a structured way. It is in no sense a test. You will score yourself. Nobody else will judge you. But you may enjoy finding out a lot more about yourself—and your career.

The Self-Discovery Wheel invites you to probe the familiar surface of your early working life—and to be honest about yourself. Honesty always pays in life—especially when that life is your own!

You are challenged to think critically but positively about yourself in six carefully-constructed sections:

1. *Motivation*
2. *Health*
3. *Pay and other rewards*
4. *Family and friends*
5. *Leisure and non-work activities*
6. *Career plans and prospects*

The picture which emerges from this stocktaking describes how you see yourself at present. What you discover about yourself—and what you do about it—is entirely up to you. If you're reasonably satisfied, you may do very little. If, however, you're less than satisfied, you may seek professional career counselling, such as that offered by *Career Choice and Job Search*.[1]

*To discover how well you're managing your life and your career, begin to score yourself.*

---

[1] *Career Choice and Job Search* is an independent career counselling service, offering continuing confidential employment counselling to college graduates and other qualified professionals. For brochure and further information, contact Sander Meredeen at 5 Crown Gardens, Dowanhill, Glasgow G12 9HJ, or call 041–357–2819.

## HOW TO SCORE YOURSELF

Remember, nobody but you will see your scores, unless you choose to share them. Try to be as honest as possible. Don't give the answer which you think is expected, but the truth about yourself as you see it.

In each of the following six sections, there are ten statements. As you work your way through these statements, score yourself as follows:

Score **5 points** if ... This statement is nearly always true.
Score **4 points** if ... This statement is often true.
Score **3 points** if ... This statement is sometimes true.
Score **2 points** if ... This statement is seldom true.
Score **1 point** if ... This statement is never true.

### Section (1) *MOTIVATION*

1. ... I'm highly motivated and set out for work each morning with a light step and a cheerful heart.
2. ... I know what I want to get out of each day's work.
3. ... I derive genuine satisfaction from the job I do.
4. ... I have lots of creative energy to give to my work.
5. ... I'm excited by the challenges which my work brings.
6. ... I'm willing to put in extra hours if the job so requires.
7. ... I learn something new every day from my job.
8. ... I can't imagine being bored or frustrated in my job.
9. ... I can see exactly where my present job is leading me.
10. ... I mostly enjoy the company of those with whom I work.

   Total score for MOTIVATION
   (50)  (Maximum possible score)

### Section (2) *HEALTH*

1. ... I know that I am primarily responsible for my own health.
2. ... I know that my work contributes positively to my health.
3. ... I have no signs that my physical health is a problem.
4. ... I am satisfied with my present body weight and shape.
5. ... I take regular physical exercise to keep myself fit.
6. ... I have full control over the amount of alcohol I consume.
7. ... I know that I eat the right combination of healthy foods.
8. ... I understand that my emotional security supports my work.
9. ... I can manage my work pressures and do not suffer stress.
▷ 10. ... I have untapped reserves of physical and mental energy.

Total score for HEALTH
(50)   (Maximum possible score)

**Section (3)** *PAY AND OTHER REWARDS*

**1.** ...   I'm satisfied with the pay I get for the work I do.
**2.** ...   I know that pay is not the most important job reward.
**3.** ...   I earn enough money to support the lifestyle I want.
**4.** ...   I know I could earn more money if I wanted to.
**5.** ...   I can pay my way and know where my money goes.
**6.** ...   I have an effective savings plan which works for me.
**7.** ...   I am not envious of others who earn more than me.
**8.** ...   I do not confuse my personal worth with what I earn.
**9.** ...   I recognize the value of fringe benefits in employment.
**10.** ...   I value the regularity of my income.

Total score for PAY AND OTHER REWARDS
(50)   (Maximum possible score)

**Section (4)** *LEISURE AND OTHER NON-WORK INTERESTS*

**1.** ...   I have enough time and energy to enjoy my leisure.
**2.** ...   I still enjoy some long-standing out-of-work interests.
**3.** ...   I enjoy adding to my present range of leisure interests.
**4.** ...   I know my leisure activities refresh me for my work.
**5.** ...   I have lots of unfulfilled leisure aims.
**6.** ...   I know that I'm not a 'workaholic'.
**7.** ...   I take my full holiday entitlement every year.
**8.** ...   I balance my active and my passive leisure activities.
**9.** ...   I work hard at my leisure interests.
**10.** ...   I regularly read for pleasure.

Total score for LEISURE AND NON-WORK ACTIVITIES
(50)   (Maximum possible score)

**Section (5)** *FAMILY AND FRIENDS*

**1.** ...   I maintain good long-term relationships with my family.
**2.** ...   I enjoy making new friends.
**3.** ...   I understand the difference between using and abusing friendship.
**4.** ...   I give my family a fair share of my time and energy.
**5.** ...   I know I can count on my friends in times of difficulty.
**6.** ...   I communicate openly with my family and friends.
▷ **7.** ...   I have always provided adequately for my family.

**8.** ...  I need my family and they need me.

**9.** ...  I count some of my work colleagues amongst my friends.

**10.** ...  I respect the right of my family to differ from me.

Total score on FAMILY AND FRIENDS

(50)   (Maximum possible score)

**Section (6)** *CAREER PLANS AND PROSPECTS*

**1.** ...  I have independent evidence of how well I perform in my present job.

**2.** ...  I know that I'm responsible for my own career planning.

**3.** ...  I have a clear view of my career needs and wants.

**4.** ...  I know how my life values are related to my career.

**5.** ...  I know what my next career move should be.

**6.** ...  I take regular stock of my career plan.

**7.** ...  I have a current *curriculum vitae* ready for use.

**8.** ...  I feel confident in facing my next employment interview.

**9.** ...  I take regular stock of the job market I'm in.

**10.** ...  I know that I'm in the right career.

Total score on CAREER PLANS AND PROSPECTS

(50)   (Maximum possible score)

HOW WELL DID YOU DO?

You've done the work. Now total up your scores. The maximum possible score for each section is 50 points.

MORE THAN 40 POINTS suggests you are managing your career well.
LESS THAN 30 POINTS suggests you are not.
LESS THAN 35 POINTS suggests you may need to seek career advice.

NOW FILL IN YOUR SELF-DISCOVERY WHEEL (Figure 16.1)

Shade the relevant segments of the *Self-Discovery Wheel* to reflect your scores. When all six segments have been shaded, consider what the *Self-Discovery Wheel* tells you about your life and your career.

Is the wheel well-balanced?
Will it take your career where you want it to go?
Is your career wheel in a rut?
Are you managing your career well?
Do you need to consider confidential career counselling?

*Career Choice and Job Search* is available to offer advice and help. For further information, call Sander Meredeen on 041–357–2819.

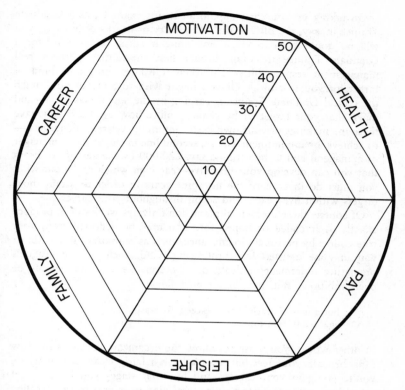

*Figure 16.1.* Self-discovery wheel © Sander Meredeen (1989)

## DEVELOPING YOUR OWN CAREER PLAN

The Bolsheviks had a word for it—where we have three—the Five-Year Plan. Of course, it has quite different aims—and it's bound to work a lot better than theirs! But in all essentials, the model is similar and it works like this. You take stock of your life at regular intervals, noting significant changes in your physical and mental health and well-being. You check your spiritual and emotional assets as well as your financial assets. You note your successes and take remedial action to correct your weaknesses and deficiencies. Above all, you set yourself clear, ambitious yet realistic targets whose achievement you then proceed to monitor on a regular basis.

On taking up your first appointment, for example, as a Graduate Trainee in, say, the BBC or the oil industry or Marks & Spencer, you will no doubt wish to know how long it takes, on average, for a Graduate Trainee to attain his/her first substantive post of real management responsibility. This then translates into some kind of target for you to aim at. Or you might wish to find out how much the typical Graduate Trainee is earning by the age of, say, 30 — and make that your target. If by chance you're now aged 25, you have there the makings of your own clear, ambitious yet realistic targets — to achieve an appointment as, say, second line manager (i.e. a manager of managers) and to be earning, say, £20 000 by the age of 30. From that you can develop your first Five-Year Plan which spells out what you must do in each of the next five years in order to attain those targets within five years. And so on throughout your career.

Of course, these theoretical plans don't always work out in practice exactly as intended or hoped for. You may be deflected from your true course by personal circumstance, such as temporary ill-health, or you may be assisted by a following wind, such as a colleague's premature retirement or death or whatever. Or you may simply be over-ambitious. But then, as the poet sings:

Ah, but a man's[2] reach should exceed his grasp,
Or what's a heaven for?

In other words, you must not allow the organizational grass to grow rank beneath your feet but always have a fairly clear idea of where you're going in your career—and by what stages you hope to get there. You can then amend your career plan from year to year, scaling your ambitions up or down, in the light of adventitious circumstances.

Another important consideration to bear in mind in the early stages of your career is whether or not to seek entry into one of several *professional associations*, and if so, which ones. If you're a mechanical or civil or electrical engineer, a lawyer or a doctor, you'll have little choice in the matter—since membership of the relevant professional body is an essential condition of your being allowed to practise in that profession. In the case of other occupational specializations—e.g. Personnel Management—you will have to consider whether or not to apply for membership of the relevant professional body (i.e. the Institute of Personnel Management).

---

[2] Robert Browning might well have included women, were he writing in 1989 instead of 1889.

*The benefits of professional membership*, especially in the early years of your career, are considerable and should not be underestimated:

- **1.** You may attend branch meetings, hear speakers, meet colleagues from other organizations and so keep yourself informed of the latest policy issues and developments in your chosen career field.

- **2.** You may receive the journal and other publications of the professional body and so keep in touch with technical developments as well as the job market in your chosen career field.

- **3.** You may, in the fullness of time, stand for office in the professional body and so come to serve younger entrants into the profession—as well as helping to advance your own career interests at the same time.

Again, throughout these early years of your career, you should take eager advantage of every opportunity provided by your employer to attend internal (or external) management training and development courses, seminars and workshops. These may be company-specific or job-specific or they may cover broad management topics—such as time management, or management development, or strategic planning, or whatever. Remember, too, that every time your own line manager is away on such a training programme, you may have an opportunity to demonstrate your capacity to deputize for him/her and so to shine.

By now, you may be wondering: Is it all worth it? The answer to that question must be a very personal matter. Nobody is in charge of your career but you. You may rise like a lark ascending on a thermal; you may be content to browse your way slowly through the peaceful valleys of life; you may be ruthlessly ambitious—and come a cropper before you're 30. These are matters of temperament, of inner drives or needs.

Beware of driving yourself—or of allowing others to drive you— farther or faster than you think desirable or worthwhile. Your employers may consider you a high flyer and generate great plans to have you transported into the organizational stratosphere. But it's up to you to nominate the altitude at which you know you function best. Take a calculated risk, by all means—you never know until you try. Be bold and adventurous, certainly. You may think there's only one way to go—and that's up. But as the title of a book recently made clear: Up Is Not The Only Way.[3] Have confidence in your own ability

---

[3] B. L. Kaye: *Up Is Not The Only Way*, Englewood Cliffs, NY: Prentice Hall (1982).

to stick at it and see it through. There's nothing quite like the feeling of satisfaction which comes from tackling the impossible—especially when you almost bring it off! But pay some attention to what your heart and stomach are telling you—as well as what your head is saying.

There comes a point in the careers of most graduates—say at around the age of 30—at which they need to consider carefully *whether to undertake a postgraduate qualification*—a second degree, a postgraduate diploma, or whatever. If you're fortunate, your employer may encourage you to think about this. At the very best, you may be sponsored to *spend a full year at a Business School, taking a Masters in Business Administration*—on the clear or implicit assumption that you will bring back your newly-acquired expertise and make it available to the organization. But that chance will be rare.

More often, you will find it necessary to take your MBA via *the part-time route* – which normally means attending lectures on two evenings per week and undertaking a great deal of reading and writing. That's tough—especially if your family and/or colleagues are encouraging you to be more socially active. The commitment to part-time study makes considerable demands on you—and on your family or your partner, if you live with one. But the intellectual rewards are great and, in career terms, you'll never regret having taken your MBA— once it's all behind you!

There's third route to an MBA—a route of growing popularity—namely, *distance learning*. This means that you don't attend lectures but work at your own pace throughout the year, receiving and returning assignments by mail, with perhaps one or two weekends spent at some designated study centre. The distance-learning route is particularly attractive to students who live well outside the acceptable evening commuting distance from a local study centre.

Yet a fourth route to an MBA may be found in the idea—now slowly catching on in the UK—of *an 'In-company MBA'*, designed and tailored to suit the organization's needs, after careful discussion between the employer and members of the Business School concerned. This arguably represents *the best of all possible worlds*—since it provides a route to an independently-recognized public qualification and yet much of the work centres upon, and is directly relevant to, your present organization.

In this whole area of personal growth and career development, what matters above all to this writer is that you *learn to understand your own needs* and *come to terms with your own limitations*—and are then ready to *mould and shape your career according to life's changing circumstances.* What seems an enjoyably hectic career lifestyle at 25 may become intolerable by the time your're thirty-something—just as the unmarried settle down to a different but no less enjoyable domestic lifestyle when they marry and have children.

At 20, you may wish to seize Fate by the lapels and shake it till the buttons fly—and the world applauds. At 40, you may seek an altogether quieter satisfaction in a variety of different outlets for your energy— of which your career is only one, and not necessarily the most important.

Finally, remember this: your work, your job and your career all constitute important aspects of your life and your enjoyment of living. They may indeed become your central life interest. But *your work and your career are not the whole of life and do not necessarily represent its most important dimensions* and should never be construed as such.

## SUGGESTIONS FOR FURTHER READING

N. Nicholson and T. Glynn-Jones: 'Good and Bad Practices in Graduate Development', in *Personnel Management*, February 1987.

# Appraising your job performance

*Between vague wavering Capability and fixed indubitable Performance, what a difference!*

Thomas Carlyle (1795–1881): *Sartor Resartus*

Chapter 17 tries to do three things:

1. To explain why you need to appraise your job performance.
2. To explore the notion of self-appraisal.
3. To suggest ways of improving your job performance.

Suppose you were to be cast away alone on a semi-tropical desert island—nobody knows for how long. How much would you bother about your appearance? If you're an adult male, would you shave every morning?—assuming, that is, you could muster a sharp razor and a modicum of sea-foam. If you're a woman, how often would you wash your hair? Or wear make-up? Or paint your finger- and toe-nails?—always assuming you'd come ashore with your vanity—and your vanity case—intact.

These questions are not as ridiculous as they might seem—for we're dealing here with *the crucial issue of personal standards*. Who sets those standards—and who monitors them—but you yourself? Ah, you say, that's not always the case. At college, for example, it's the Dean and Faculty who set the performance standard—the pass mark—not the students. That's perfectly true. But the standard itself has emerged from years of observing the work performance of Average, Below-

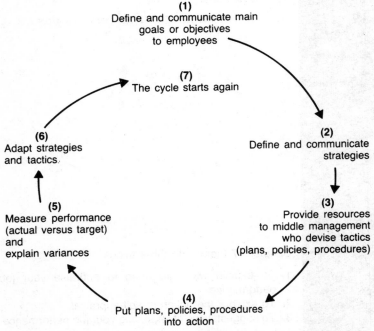

*Figure 17.1.* The virtuous circle of productive enterprise

Average, and Above-Average students. Those observations, in turn, have enabled the Dean and Faculty to calibrate a set of reasonably reliable benchmarks for what constitutes an 'acceptable' level of academic performance by an 'average' student in any given subject in any year.

What's true of college is even more true of paid employment—namely, that *you must expect your work performance to be assessed against certain rigorously defined standards*. What are those standards in paid employment—and who does the assessing?

Despite many superficial differences—for example, in job content and methods of working—those responsible for managing productive enterprise, whether profit-centred or not, whether in industry, commerce or the service sector, are all engaged in essentially the same broad managerial functions (see Figure 17.1 above).

The 'virtuous circle of productive enterprise' is there conceptualized as comprising seven key management tasks:

o 1. To define and communicate the organization's main goals to subordinate employees.

o 2. To define and communicate the strategies by which the organization will achieve all or most of its objectives.

o 3. To provide the resources which enable subordinates to turn strategies into tactics by developing plans, policies and procedures to achieve those objectives.

o 4. To put plans, policies and procedures into action.

o 5. To measure performance (i.e. actual performance against planned or targetted performance) and to explain variances.

o 6. To adapt strategies and tactics in order to correct adverse variances.

o 7. To manage the next cycle better than the last one.

## THE PURPOSE OF JOB PERFORMANCE APPRAISAL

What especially concerns us here is (5) above—namely, the inescapable duty—which falls on the shoulders of managers everywhere—of measuring or appraising the *actual performance* of subordinates against a predetermined *target* or *set of performance standards*—and of explaining the negative/positive variances.

Please note that the duty is 'inescapable' and that the object of the exercise is to 'explain' variances rather than to punish those whose work performance is being appraised. 'Inescapable' because wherever men and women engage in any worthwhile enterprise, there is a felt need to assess how well or how badly they perform, either in their own eyes or those of their peers or their bosses. Without some assessment, some measurement of how well we're doing against some predefined standard, we lack any real sense of achievement and so risk losing our vital motivation.

Once we have set up those predefined standards, we can begin to explain any adverse variances in our actual performance and then go on to correct or improve our subsequent performance so as to match or surpass our previous best standards.

The simplest analogy is perhaps with athletics. Every serious athlete carries around in his/her head two well-defined standards—a 'personal best' and then some local, national or international standard. All serious athletes pit themselves against either or both those standards whenever they take the field in their chosen event. It's only by doing so that they can ever hope to maintain—and eventually surpass—their own personal best. And what's true for athletic performance applies with equal force to every kind of job performance.

All measurement or appraisal of current job performance is essentially *future-oriented*, in the sense that it seeks to improve future performance. In the words of a leading study, the purposes of job performance appraisal may be described as follows:

- 1. *To improve* organizational effectiveness:
  (a) by encouraging the setting of job targets jointly by employees and their managers, against which future performance can be assessed;
  (b) by encouraging managers to consider and determine with their employees what additional skill requirements are necessary to meet present job demands, and future demands arising from, for example, changes in technology and legislation;
  (c) and by encouraging managers to consider employee succession.

- 2. *To give* employees a better appreciation of their managers' expectations of their performance and, at the same time, to acquaint managers with subordinates' expectations of them.

- 3. *To alert* managers to constraints which may be inhibiting employee performance.

- 4. *To improve* employee job satisfaction through the activation of their first three objectives.[1]

---

[1] Gordon Anderson, David Hulme and Ed Young: 'Appraisal without form-filling', in *Personnel Management*, February 1987.

# HOW PERFORMANCE APPRAISAL WORKS IN PRACTICE?

There are an infinite variety of different ways in which organizations set about the systematic appraisal of employee job performance. Underlying this superficial diversity of approach there nevertheless lies a conceptual unity—since all valid appraisal schemes must seek to cover the following eight key points:

- **1.** It's important to identify *certain personal details* about the named employee who is the subject of this particular appraisal (e.g. age, grade, job title, length of time in post, period covered by the appraisal, date of appraisal, etc.).

- **2.** It's essential for the appraiser to identify clearly and succinctly the employee's *major work objectives* during the period of the appraisal; and to say whether those objectives are assessed as having been:
  (i)   Not met
  (ii)  Met
  (iii) Exceeded.

- **3.** Insofar as major work objectives have *not* been met, it's extremely useful for the manager who carries out the appraisal to say whether there were any *special circumstances* which may help to explain those failures to meet objectives.

- **4.** It's necessary to make some assessment of the individual's performance against each of a number of predefined *Job Demands* using a predefined and calibrated scale of performance standards—for example:

| Job Demands | *Performance Standards* |
| --- | --- |
| | N/A  U  M  S  SP  E  O |
| 1. Administrative skills | |
| 2. Communication skills—written | |
| 3. Communication skills—verbal | |
| 4. Problem analysis | |
| 5. Decision making | |
| 6. Delegation | |
| 7. Quantity of work | |
| 8. Development of personnel | |
| 9. Development of quality improvements | |

*Key:* N/A = Not applicable    S = Satisfactory
     U = Unsatisfactory    SP = Satisfactory Plus
     M = Marginal    E = Excellent
         O = Outstanding

- 5. It's necessary to make some assessment of the individual's perform-ance against each of a number of *Personal Characteristics* using a predefined and calibrated set of performance standards—as follows:

| Personal Characteristics | Performance Standards | | | | |
|---|---|---|---|---|---|
| | 1 | 2 | 3 | 4 | 5 |
| 1. Initiative | | | | | |
| 2. Persistence | | | | | |
| 3. Ability to work with others | | | | | |
| 4. Adaptability | | | | | |
| 5. Persuasiveness | | | | | |
| 6. Self-confidence | | | | | |
| 7. Judgement | | | | | |
| 8. Leadership | | | | | |
| 9. Creativity | | | | | |

Note: Most Performance Standards lend themselves to assessment within a five-fold qualitative or, as here, quantitative range.

- 6. It's extremely helpful for the manager carrying out the appraisal to highlight those *specific Performance Factors and Personal Character-istics* which are considered to be the employee's *major strengths/limitations* and which have significantly affected job performance in the period covered by the appraisal.

- 7. It's highly desirable, though perhaps not essential, for *some Overall Performance rating* to be given, which takes full account of the assessments made under each of the above headings.

- 8. It is absolutely essential *to identify the manager who has carried out the appraisal* and to add some carefully worded signed statement to the effect that: 'This Performance Appraisal has been carried out in a fair and impartial manner and is based on the work performance of the employee during the period under review in this appraisal'.

## WHAT ABOUT SELF-APPRAISAL?

Appraisal systems of the type so far described are frequently carried out without the prior knowledge or involvement of the employees being appraised. In the past, most employers required their managers to conduct employee performance appraisal as a type of secret ritual. Hardly surprising, therefore, that the leading researchers into appraisal schemes conclude that the performance of those schemes fall far short of their initial promise:

Although the objectives of performance appraisal are accepted as being praiseworthy and utilitarian, it is well documented that the great majority of schemes have not lived up to expectations.[2]

Having belatedly recognized that the whole point of appraisal is not simply to judge but to encourage improved work performance, most progressive employers now require their managers to carry out *open appraisal*—i.e. to appraise their subordinates in ways which completely involve the employee him/herself.

*Open appraisal* is intended to ensure that there are *mutually agreed work goals or objectives* which are clear, realistic (i.e. attainable), consistent, controllable, challenging and significant for reasons which should be made clear to both the employee and the appraising manager. This implies that there must be a series of face-to-face interviews at which employees are invited to say how well they consider they have performed their work in the period under appraisal.

## SELF-APPRAISAL CHECKLIST

1. What were the main tasks which you set out to achieve?
2. Which of these tasks do you feel you have achieved: (a) fully, (b) partially, (c) not at all?
3. Which aspects of your job do you feel you have done best?
4. Which aspects of your job do you feel you have done least well?
5. What special factors, if any, intervened to reduce your work performance over the last appraisal period?
6. What do you feel your work objectives should be over the next appraisal period?
7. What further training do you feel you need to help you improve your work performance?
8. In what ways, if any, would you wish to see your work restructured in order to improve overall organizational performance?
9. Are there any other matters relevant to your performance which you wish to discuss with your manager during your performance appraisal interview?

The *self-appraisal check-list* of questions is intended to stimulate your thinking. This checklist provides an invaluable preparation for performance appraisal interviews because it encourages employees to take a more realistic view of their past and their future work performance. So, if you're due to take part in your first performance appraisal interview, the best way to prepare yourself is to review

[2] Anderson, Hulme and Young: *loc. cit.*

systematically the questions in the above checklist. You will then meet your manager at the appraisal interview on more equal terms. What's more, in planning your future workload you should have the opportunity of putting forward your own views and so have the psychological satisfaction of 'owning' at least some part of your own future work performance targets.

Once more, *an important note of caution* is required. The performance appraisal interview does *not* represent a meeting of equals. There's no place for sentiment or personal feelings at performance appraisal interview. However pleasant and considerate your boss might seem (or even be!), she/he is appraising a subordinate in accordance with organization policy and should therefore be following laid-down procedure. Whilst there may be some scope for compromise in determining future workloads and tasks, there should be no compromise when it comes to performance standards.

## HOW TO IMPROVE YOUR JOB PERFORMANCE

There are a number of ways in which you can evaluate and improve your job performance ahead of your next performance appraisal:

- *First*, when starting a new job, it's a good idea to maintain a brief written log of all the tasks you're asked to carry out, together with your running comments on points learned or observations made along the way. By doing this, you not only derive a greater sense of achievement at how far you've come in your early weeks and months in the job; you'll also have a more detailed recall of the points you might wish to raise when you sit down with your manager to take informal (or formal) stock of how you're doing.

- *Second*, you should soon recognize where your existing qualifications and skills fall short of what you'll need to maintain even a satisfactory performance in your new job. Make sure you keep good notes on the subject areas in which you feel you need further training. Use these notes at your next progress review with your manager, to back your request for the additional training you feel you need.

- *Third*, learn the difficult art of pacing yourself at work so that you keep going all day, the whole working week. The trick is to conserve your physical and mental enegy so that you do not exhaust yourself or suffer premature 'burn-out'. Good health should not be taken for granted. So, learn to take care of yourself—and be all you can be.

- *Fourth*, when you come up against work-related problems that appear insoluble, try viewing them from a new angle—for example, by standing on your head. Better still, try standing the problems on their head. You'd be amazed how often a new angle reveals fresh possibilities. Once mastered, this is a technique which can help you improve your work performance throughout your working life.

- *Fifth*, *do* try to keep a sense of proportion about the problems which inevitably afflict your early career. A problem which appears insoluble at midnight may become transparently clear with a self-evident solution at dawn, after a good night's sleep. On the other hand, if you've a Monday 9 a.m. deadline to meet, it usually pays to work all day Saturday to crack the problem rather than still be working at it through a sleepless Sunday night!

### SUGGESTIONS FOR FURTHER READING

Gordon Anderson, David Hulme and Ed Young: 'Appraisal without form-filling', in *Personnel Management*, February 1987.

Kenneth R. Robinson: *Effective performance review techniques: a self-help guide*, London: Institute of Personnel Management (1983).

Derek Torrington and Laura Hall: *Personnel Management: A New Approach*, London: Prentice-Hall (1987) Chapter 4: 'Performance assessment and the appraisal interview'.

# chapter

# 18

# High flyers and the Icarus complex

*Climb high*

*Climb far*

*Your goal the sky*

*Your aim the star*

   Inscription on Hopkins Memorial Steps, Williams

   College, Williamstown, Massachusetts

Chapter 18 tries to do three things:

1. To present some profiles of high flyers.
2. To encourage potential high flyers to soar.
3. To warn you against the fate of Icarus.

# REACH FOR THE SKIES!

The 50th anniversary of the outbreak of the Second World War is much on this author's mind at this time of writing. We who were young then and who lived through the Battle of Britain recall with gratitude the ardent heroism and selfless sacrifice of those young Spitfire and Hurricane pilots—high flyers indeed!—who fought and won those single-handed combats in the skies above southern Britain—against insuperable odds. They were not supermen but ordinary people—called through glory, to the stars.

As in war, so in peace. In every walk of life, in every field of endeavour, you'll find those who, for whatever combination of reasons, seem destined to accomplish far more than might reasonably be expected of them. Who are these high flyers? How and why do they achieve so much more than most of their contemporaries? And what lessons are there for the rest of us?

### Sir Campbell Adamson's story

Born in 1922, only son of an Edinburgh Chartered Accountant, he was sent pre-war to Rugby School, and thence to wartime Cambridge where he studied economics with Joan Robinson, a distinguished marxist. Resisting her powerful ideological influence, he graduated in 1944, did a brief stint in International Affairs at Chatham House, and in 1945 joined Baldwins Ltd as a steel industry management trainee.

Over the next 24 years he rose to become a Director (1959–69) of the nationalized steel combine, Richard Thomas & Baldwins Ltd, and General Manager (1961–1967) in charge of the construction and commissioning of Britain's last great integrated steelworks at Llanwern, Mon.

Seconded to the Department of Economic Affairs (1967–1969), he assisted the formidable George Brown to launch the ill-fated National Economic Plan, intended to regenerate Britain's flagging economy. From 1969–1976 he was an invigorating and respected Director General of the CBI, responsible for putting that organization on the national map for the first time.

> Knighted (1976) for services to industry, he served in turn as Director of the Imperial Group, Lazard Brothers, Doulton & Co., and Tarmac plc. Elected Chairman of Abbey National in 1978, he pioneered its flotation as a plc in 1988–1989.
>
> Vice-Chairman (1975–1977) of the National Savings Committee, he was on the BBC Advisory Committee; NEDC; the Design Council; SSRC; Council, the Industrial Society; was Visiting Fellow, Lancaster University and Nuffield College, Oxford and a Governor of Rugby School. Married twice, with four children, he lists his hobbies as brass-rubbing, tennis, music—and arguing!

As this profile of Sir Campbell Adamson implicitly demonstrates, we are certainly not born equal—in physique, intelligence, strength, appetite, taste or ambition. Whilst some will settle down happily on the lower slopes of modest achievement, others are driven to scale ever-higher peaks. Some of us are A-Type personalities, inner-directed, high-achievers, never still, always striving for perfection, at work and at play; others are B-Types, more willing to rest on our laurels, neglect our commissions, hang up our boots, go fishing, grow roses.

## ARE YOU A HIGH FLYER?

It's vital that you discover your own true nature and work with the grain of your own personality. If you're a natural A-Type in a B-Type job, you'll fret and fume until you get promotion or break out of it. If you're a B-Type forced into an A-Type job, the chances are you won't break *out* so much as break *down* under its stresses and strains. High flyers are frequently A-Type personalities whose distinctive leadership traits emerge early in life and which persist throughout their subsequent careers.

> **ARE YOU A HIGH FLYER?**
> High Flyers exhibit clear distinguishing features. Do you possess any or all of their indispensable gifts?
> 1. To function well with relatively little sleep.
> 2. To work best under severe pressure.
> 3. To mobilize and discharge unusual amounts of psychic energy.
> 4. To recover relatively easily from mistakes.
> 5. To learn from both positive and negative experience.
> 6. To organize others into getting things done to a very high standard of performance.

Incidentally, it's quite fallacious to imagine that high flyers lead charmed lives and suffer no major set-backs. Campbell Adamson carried the can for various corporate errors at Llanwern; was unlucky enough to work for the bibulous George Brown; and, as Director General at the CBI, was held largely responsible for the Heath Government's four-day working week in 1971; and the disappointing early leaks sprung in the Abbey National flotation in mid-1989. His career does not seem to have suffered unduly!

John Harvey-Jones is another high flyer who knows something about success and set-back. He worked his way up from graduate trainee to become Chairman of ICI, Britain's biggest and most successful industrial enterprise. This is what Sir John has to say about leadership and high flyers:

> The concept of the ferryman [capable of steering us successfully from the past into the future] is also interesting but totally improbable. Who wouldn't like to know people who have [these] qualities ... I guess the reality of life will be that we just have to muddle along with the sort of evolutionary development of leadership that we have over the past years rather than believing that a new form of renaissance man is going to emerge. I think if I were a young man just starting my career in industry, I would be immensely depressed at the concept that that is what I had to be in order to rise to the top. I must consider myself lucky that I hold the job I do before these supermen have arrived![1]

### Sir John Harvey-Jones' story

Born 1924 into a comfortable family, Sir John was sent to a private school in Kent before entering the Royal Navy as a Dartmouth College cadet in 1937. Specializing in submarine warfare, he subsequently qualified as an interpreter in both Russian and German and held various posts in Naval Intelligence.

Resigning from the Navy as Lieutenant-Commander in 1956 at the age of 32, he joined ICI as a humble Work Study Officer at Wilton, working his way through various commercial appointments to become Director of Technical-Commercial oper-

---

[1] John Harvey-Jones: 'Forecasting change'—a review of Hugh Marlow's *Success: Individual, Corporate and National*, in *Personnel Management*, May 1984.

ations in 1967. He took charge of ICI's Petrochemicals Division from 1970 to 1973 when he was elected to the Main Board, served as Deputy Chairman 1978–1982 and Chairman 1982–1987.

During that period, Sir John was also Chairman of Phillips–Imperial Petroleum 1973–1975; a Non-Executive Director of Carrington–Viyella 1974–1979 and 1981–1984; of Reed International 1975–1984; of Grand Metropolitan 1983– ; of Burns Anderson 1987– ; and of others too numerous to list.

In his last years at ICI he served on the Governing Bodies of such prestigious organizations as the BIM; the Hearing & Speech Trust; Great Ormond Street Redevelopment Appeal; the Police Foundation; and the Science Museum. Elected Chancellor of Bradford University in 1986, with Honorary Degrees from many Universities, he received a Knighthood in 1985.

In 1987, the year of his nominal retirement, he published his memoirs: *Making It Happen*. Throughout his career he has found time for a formidable range of recreations which include ocean sailing, swimming, countryside pursuits, cooking, contemporary literature and pony driving.

### Richard Branson's story

*You want to be able to look back and feel fully satisfied with the conduct of your life. (Interview with Mark Milner* Financial Guardian *5 November 1986)*

Founder and Chairman of the Virgin Music Group, Richard was born in 1950. Son of a barrister and financial consultant father and grandson of a High Court judge, he was sent to Stowe School where he became interested in journalism. He went on to become Editor of *Student* magazine 1968–1969; set up the *Student Advisory Centre* (now *Help*) in 1970.

Richard founded the Virgin Mail-Order Co. in 1969, followed by Virgin Retail, Virgin Record Label, Virgin Music Publishing, Virgin Recording Studios and Virgin Airlines in 1984.

In 1986, the Virgin Group plc was floated on the Stock Exchange and the Voyager Group formed to encompass his business interests in travel, clubs and hotels.

In that same year, Richard captured popular imagination as Captain of Atlantic Challenger II, winner of the Blue Riband for the fastest crossing of the Atlantic by a ship. In 1987, he became the first man to cross the Atlantic in a hot-air balloon (with Per Lindstrand); and attained the fastest speed in a hot air balloon (140 m.p.h.) in 1987.

In 1986, Richard became Chairman of UK 2000 and a Director of Intourist Moscow Ltd in 1988. In 1987, he launched a charity, The Healthcare Foundation. Virgin Records was launched in the US in 1987.

In October 1989, Richard, who had taken his Virgin company to the Stock Exchange and brought it out again, announced that he had entered into a partnership with the Fujisankei Communications Group of Japan—part of his strategy for keeping Virgin 'independent for ever'.

### Sebastian Coe's story

One of Britain's most successful young athletes, born in 1956, Seb won his first Gold Medal for running the 1500 m and his first Silver Medal for the 800 m at the Moscow Olympics in 1980, at the age of 23. He set world records at 800 m, at 1000 m and for the mile in 1981. In recognition of his achievements, he was awarded the MBE in 1982.

Two years later, he went on to win his second Gold Medal for the 1500 m and his second Silver Medal for the 800 m, at the Los Angeles Olympics in 1984. He became the European Champion for the 800 m at Stuttgart in 1986.

Seb began his serious running career at Loughborough University where he took his BSc Honours degree in Economics and Social History in 1980, going on to become Research Assistant there from 1981 to 1984. The University conferred on him the Honorary Degree of Doctor of Technology in 1985.

Seb served as Member of the Sports Council from 1983 and became Vice Chairman in 1986. In addition, he has been a Member of the Health Education Authority and of the Medical Communication Olympic Committee since 1987.

▶ Seb jointly authored his first book *Running Free* (with David Miller) in 1981; and his second, *Running for Fitness* (with his father and trainer, Peter Coe) in 1983.

By his own admission, Seb Coe avoids all strenuous activity when away from the track. He lists his favourite recreations as listening to recorded or preferably live jazz; theatre; and reading. In September 1989, aged just 33, Seb announced his retirement from athletics.

In November 1989, Seb threw his hat into the political ring when he was adopted as Conservative candidate for the Cornish parliamentary constituency of Falmouth and Camborne.

### Simon Rattle's story

'*Mop-headed boy with a golden baton*' (Guardian)

Britain's most brilliant young orchestral conductor, Simon was born in Liverpool in 1955 and won the Bournemouth John Player International Conducting Competition at the age of 19, in 1974. Following his Festival Hall debut in 1976, he has gone on to build an outstanding international career in the fiercely competitive world of orchestral conducting.

In Britain, he has conducted the Bournemouth Sinfonietta; the Philharmonia; the Northern Sinfonia; the London Philharmonic and the London Sinfonietta.

Abroad, he has conducted the Boston Symphony; the Chicago Symphony; the Cleveland, the Concertgebouw, the Toronto and the Stockholm Philharmonic Orchestras, among others.

Following his Glasgow debut in 1976, he was Assistant Conductor, BBC Scottish Symphony Orchestra and Associate Conductor, Royal Liverpool Philharmonic Society, 1977–1980; and Principal Conductor, London Choral Society 1979–1983.

Simon was appointed Principal Conductor, City of Birmingham Symphony Orchestra in 1980, and has been Principal Guest Conductor, Los Angeles Philharmonic since 1981.

In the mid-1970s he awarded himself a sabbatical away from orchestral music and spent the academic year studying mainly history and literature at Oxford.

He was awarded the CBE for services to music in 1987.

## Martin Amis' story

*I don't see myself as as prophet. I'm not writing social comment. My books are playful literature. I'm after laughs. (Interview in* Cosmopolitan *1978)*

Regarded by many critics as the brightest talent amongst Britain's younger generation of writers, Martin was born in 1949, son of author Kingsley Amis and his first wife, Hilary Bardwell.

He was enrolled at more than a dozen schools in various parts of Europe and the United States and then a series of 'crammers' to prepare for university entrance examinations. He went on to Exeter College, Oxford, where he took 'a formal First' Class Honours Degree in English in 1973.

Since coming down, he has earned his living in a variety of literary roles. In 1974, he was appointed Fiction and Poetry Editor of the *Times Literary Supplement.* From 1977–1979 he was Literary Editor of the *New Statesman.*

A prolific writer with a prodigious talent to amuse, his first novel, *The Rachel Papers*, appeared in 1973, and won him the Somerset Maugham Award 1974). This has since been followed by: *Dead Babies* (1975), *Success* (1978), *Other People: a mystery story* (1981), *Money* (1984), *The Moronic Inferno and Other Visits to America* (1986), *Einstein's Monsters*, short stories (1987) and *London Fields* (1989).

Described by some reviewers as the author of 'wickedly clever black comedies', he has been hailed elsewhere as 'an outstanding young novelist who satirizes the scabrous excesses of youth and contemporary society and displays an irreverent and incessant wit, similar to that of his father.'

It is one thing to achieve fame or notoriety as a lively young novelist—quite another to live down a famous literary father. Martin has done both. Read him and judge for yourself.

## Diana Cornish's story

*No free lunch but Cornish cream at the top*

Although she fails to disclose her year of birth—and why should she, except on her own CV?—we know that she left school mid-term; got a job as receptionist in her grandfather's factory; learned as much as possible about the business and book-keeping by day; and went to night school to learn shorthand and typing.

Following marriage and the birth of her daughter in 1966, she returned to work full-time as a costings clerk for a Luton hat firm; continued to work part-time for her grandfather; and still found time, in the evenings, to work as an Avon Lady, selling cosmetics door-to-door and ending up with responsibility for almost 200 representatives.

Over the next 10 years, she worked her way up as a member of the salesforce of the Blue Arrow Group to become Training Manager, and was eventually promoted a Regional Director. In 1985, when Blue Arrow bought the Brook Street Employment Bureau, she persuaded her boss to allow her to transfer to the Bureau—where three years later she was appointed to the board. She became Managing Director in 1987.

Diana is a Fellow of the Institute of Employment Consultants, speaks regularly on employment matters in all areas and takes a particular interest in the issues surrounding women at work.

As her brilliant career demonstrates, leadership qualities are by no means confined to men—nor to those who've graduated from college. But promotion and success do not come automatically nor are they to be found amongst those who simply work 9 to 5. There's a price to be paid for every successful career—and there's certainly no free lunch!

### Sir Oscar de Ville's story

Born in a Derbyshire mining village, he rarely speaks of his humble origins. His natural gifts emerged at school and he might well have gone straight to Cambridge as a scholarship boy—but for the war.

Volunteering for the Royal Navy at 18, he endured the horrors of the Arctic convoys to Russia. He was later commissioned to become one of the Navy's youngest commanders in charge of his own mine-sweeper at the age of 21, after first serving in motor torpedo boats in the English Channel.

After the war, he read Russian at Cambridge and was interested in becoming a schoolmaster when he was offered a graduate traineeship at Ford Motor Company, largely on the strength, so he claimed, of his love of rugby, not his fluent Russian.

Having worked on apprentice and operator training, he was in due course appointed Company Training Manager. Latterly, as Staff Manager, he was involved with all Ford's human resource development. In 1963 he was appointed second-in-command of Ford's revolutionary strategic planning unit for better employee relations.

By 1965, he concluded that he lacked sufficient front-line negotiating experience with the Ford manual unions to become Director of Employee Relations. After 20 years, he decided to leave Ford.

Headhunted to BICC, he took charge of Employee Relations, rising meteorically to become first a Director, then Deputy Chairman, injecting further vitality and strategic planning to help achieve BICC's vastly improved performance.

Denied the BICC Chairmanship, Oscar became deputy Chairman in 1985 and Chairman in 1987 of Meyer International plc, where he continues to inspire confidence and superior performance. He was awarded a Knighthood in 1990.

## Sophie Mirman's story

*I shrug my shoulders in despair at women who moan at the lack of opportunities and then take two weeks off as a result of falling out with their boy friends. (Interview in the* Guardian *1 April 1988)*

Uncrowned 'Queen of niche market operations', Sophie is the woman entrepreneur who has literally socked it to us with The Sock Shop, a multi-million pound business which she modestly started in 1982, when she was apparently unable to buy a suitable pair of socks to go with her new white woollen dress! The company was over-subscribed 54-fold when it was floated on the Stock Market in 1987.

Now Chairman of the Sock Shop, she and her husband opened her first kiosk in London's Knightsbridge Underground station and now employ over 400 people in more than 65 outlets. Before the Sock Shop came the Tie Rack. Socks account for some 80% of the turnover, umbrellas and sundries for most of the rest.

There is no known family connection with Ethel Merman, the American *chanteuse*.

Chosen as Business Woman of the Year 1987, an award jointly sponsored by champagne house Veuve Clicquot and the Institute of Directors, Sophie has had a vine named after her in Rheims and will receive a gift of champagne on her birthday for the rest of her life. The Institute's plans for marking her birthday remain a closely-guarded secret.

Not bad going for the one-time Secretary to Marks & Spencer chief, Lord Sieff! The M & S management development scheme clearly failed to detect her ambition or to appreciate her outstanding flair for business. But then, working for a huge corporation, like M & S, is not everybody's idea of an enjoyable career—and long-term, it was certainly not Sophie's choice.

**Anita Roddick's story**

*I don't want to be bloody still. I say we survive on stress—I don't want to be laid back.* Sunday Times *interview 6 March 1988*

Ten years is a long work-stretch in any person's life. But when the results pay off, as they clearly have done for Anita, who counts the cost?—other than Gordon, her accountant husband.

Before she met Gordon, Anita helped her Italian parents run the family's modest café at the Sussex resort of Littlehampton. After they married, she and Gordon stayed in the food business, first running a hotel, then a hamburger restaurant.

They opened their first Body Shop in Brighton in 1976. Ten years later, the franchise operation, devised by Gordon, had spawned more than 300 Body Shops and produced an annual turnover of £28.5m.

Franchising has been described as a way of hiring a good business idea without having to dream it up for yourself. In America, franchising is still one of the fastest-growing sectors of the economy—ranging from the more traditional laundrette to hotel-keeping, from highly professional house-cleaning to less orthodox husband-sitting.

Anita is the very model of the successful modern business woman. In a *Sunday Times* interview she was described as being not just wealthy but the self-appointed exemplar of 'new age' business management. She knows her mind—and clearly speaks it: 'I don't have any fxxxing duty to [my customers] at all. My only duty is to my company and to keep it alive in a way I think is right and honest. I care more about the investment in spirit than the bloody investment in time and money.

Not quite in line with 'new age' business management or current thinking on customer care—but it's the robust language of business which everybody understands!

## COMING UNSTUCK IN YOUR EARLY CAREER

This seems a good point at which to recall the myth of Icarus, that powerful Greek metaphor which encapsulates much of our discussion in this chapter. If you've not encountered Icarus in your general reading, you may know of him from a famous painting by Breughel, which presents a stunning account of a young man's tragic fall from grace. For Icarus was the son of Daedalus, an ambitious father, who wished nothing less for his son than that he should excel above all others by soaring aloft on artificial wings—like a bird. Unfortuantely, he flew so high that he came too close to the sun—whose heat melted the wax with which his artificial wings were fastened in place—and plunged tragically into the Aegean. Hence the myth which is inseparably linked to his name.

Each year, we're reminded of Icarus when a number of high flyers, in all fields of employment, plunge ignominiously to earth after flying too close to the sun. As usual, the Greeks had a word for it—*hubris*—that supreme arrogance which is rewarded by the humiliation which eventually comes to all those who forget they are merely mortal and who seek the lifestyle of the gods. Yuppies beware!

If, through the genetic jackpot, you've been fortunate enough to inherit some superior gifts or talents, you should obviously want to make the most of them. There are always plenty of organizations willing to hire you in order to help them solve *their* problems. The trick, with respect, is to ensure they don't simply add to *yours*! The last thing you should do with talent is to squander it recklessly and so risk burn-out or some other serious psychological trauma before you're 30.

Just as there are organizations that assist parents who are blessed with a so-called 'gifted child', perhaps there should be an organization which helps high flyers come to terms with the risks and opportunities conferred on them by their superior gifts and which helps them to deal with their repercussive effects. In short, unless they're counselled against the risks, high flyers may push themselves too far, too fast. They are also liable to be exploited by some unscrupulous employers and could be forced to fly too high, too soon—even for high flyers.

If you're a potential high flyer who's earthbound or who's still hedge-hopping—why not extend your wings and fly? You've nothing to lose but your humility. As you soar aloft, keep a sharp look-out for larger birds of prey coming out of the sun. And keep a close eye on your altimeter—before your wings begin to melt!

*Good luck—and successful soaring—as you reach for the skies!*

## SUGGESTIONS FOR FURTHER READING

Political and Economic Planning: *Thrusters and Sleepers*, London: Allen & Unwin (1965).

# Moving up—or moving on?

*A man with a career can have no time to waste upon his wife and friends; he has to devote it wholly to his enemies.*

John Oliver Holmes (1867–1906)

Chapter 19 tries to do three things:

1. To invite you to promote your own early career.
2. To suggest how to tackle some early career crises.
3. To help you make the most of an early career move.

## WHO'S PROMOTING YOUR EARLY CAREER?

Ever noticed what happens when Eurythmics come to town? Although they've been top of the pops for almost a decade, their arrival is preceded by an avalanche of publicity. In short, they continue to pay their agents good money to promote their careers and so ensure their continuing success. Surely, there's a lesson for us there, somewhere!

During your final year at college—and after graduation—you work hard to ensure you miss no opportunity to promote your unborn career. There's no lack of pre-natal care. Once your career is born, however, there's often a lack of continuing, post-natal care. Consequently, many an infant career expires prematurely in its early weeks or months. How do you prevent that happening to *your* career in its first tender months?

It's easy to understand this neglect. You've put so much of yourself into securing that first paid appointment, you've consumed so much energy, it seems only natural to relax and take things a little easier for a while. You really can't afford to do this. Not if you value your career.

## FOUR SIMPLE STEPS TO HELP YOU SUCCEED

So, what's to be done? We'd like to suggest that you consider adopting four simple procedures in the first months of your career:

- 1. Maintain a daily work planner.
- 2. Practice good time management.
- 3. Keep a regular work log.
- 4. Extract the lessons from each week's work.

If you make these procedures part of your regular work routine, we promise you your career will prosper, your prospects will be enhanced—and the routines will stand you in good stead throughout the rest of your career.

### MAINTAIN A DAILY WORK PLANNER

Whatever your early morning routines—whether or not you say your prayers; go jogging; do yoga; eat or do not eat breakfast—find five minutes every morning, before you leave home, to plan your key work tasks for the day ahead. Bring forward tasks left undone from the previous work day. Add new tasks. And give them a fresh priority—new every morning—thus:

*Tuesday 10 April 1990*

| | | |
|---|---|---|
| xx | 1. | Call Ian Easton *re* Oakley Terrace |
| x | 2. | Order continuous stationery for Amstrad |
| xxx | 3. | Fix urgent meeting with Barbara Cohen |
| xxx | 4. | Buy and send birthday card to Eli |
| xx | 5. | Research last month's budget overspend |
| x | 6. | Reply to John Midgley's invitation |
| x | 7. | Investigate policy on travel allowances |
| xxx | 8. | Transfer cash from Abbey to Clydesdale |
| x | 9. | Reserve tickets for La Bohème Tuesday 24/4 |
| x | 10. | Complete tax return |
| x | 11. | Meet Eli 7 pm at Shish |
| xx | 12. | Call Mordechai Richler |

Keep this planner close to hand throughout the day, attending always to your three-star, highest-priority tasks first. Enjoy the sense of achievement as you delete each high priority task accomplished. Add new tasks for inclusion in tomorrow's listing. Keep up the good work!

## PRACTICE GOOD TIME MANAGEMENT

Learn to conserve, manage and make the best use of the scarcest and most valuable of your resources—Time. Here are six tips for better time management:

o *Keep a 'time diary'* for a typical working week, showing how you currently spend each hour of your working day (e.g. reading; at meetings; telephoning; writing; waiting; resting; chatting; thinking; thinking?!).

o *Analyse the resulting diary* for your total use of time and decide whether you're using your time wisely, productively, creatively.

o *Adjust the future use of your time* to ensure that you reduce or eliminate waste. Cut out as much waiting time as possible. Try listing all your phone calls and deal with them at one sitting. If possible, try to handle each letter or other piece of paper once only.

o *Maintain and increase your productivity* by building regular work breaks, regular exercise periods, and sensible eating and drinking into your work diary.

○ *Watch out for work pressures* which threaten to generate stress—and deal with them intelligently before they impair your work performance.

○ *Be chivalrous with people: be ruthless with time.* Don't cut your family and friends. Give them your premium time, if you possibly can. Don't ask more of your colleagues than you know they can give. Be merciless in terms of your own time management.

## KEEP A REGULAR WORK LOG

In Chapter 9 on Job Search, we suggested you keep a log of all the jobs for which you were applying, with a clear set of notes on the outcome of each job application. We now suggest you start a new log for a new job. All you need is a small exercise book, or page-a-day diary, and 15 minutes towards the end of each day. And a smidgeon of self-discipline!

You should aim to sit down quietly each evening, for just 15 minutes, to capture your sharpest impressions of that day. Not simply a diary of key people, dates and events, but some frank, evaluative commentary on what you've observed; the lessons learned; the policy issues you've encountered; the problems unresolved; the matters you plan to follow up and review before your next job performance appraisal. Each weekend, when you ransack, clip and throw out the week's old newspapers, go through your log for that week and add your own brief marginal comments in another colour: 'Nonsense!' 'Follow up!' 'Link up with XYZ!' 'Compare ABC!'

## TALK THROUGH YOUR WORK PROBLEMS

Seek to maintain a lively, mutually rewarding, confidential dialogue with a trusted friend or one or two carefully selected colleagues—a fellow graduate trainee; a member of your work team; even your immediate supervisor or Training Adviser.

Carry on this discussion on a fairly regular basis (e.g. try to have lunch together once or twice a week). Be serious but try not to become too solemn or self-conscious about it. Select any single critical incident during your past week's work which went less well than you might have wished. Describe the situation factually and unemotionally. Then discuss your reactions to it. Be sharply critical, by all means. Invite comments and suggestions for alternative ways of handling any difficulties which may have arisen. Share problems and solutions. Always play the ball, not the player.

Finally, if you adopt these four simple procedures, and nothing more, you'll have an excellent set of manuscript notes towards the biographical analysis of your career to date, ready for use whenever you need to write it up. But there's much more you can do to nurture your infant career by tackling problems before they become the source of a career crisis.

## HOW TO COPE WITH EARLY CAREER CRISES

Once you recognize that the career path—like the path of true love— never did run smooth, you won't be too dejected when you come up against your first career crisis. Here are some of the most frequently reported problems which may become the source of an early career crisis:

1. *My boss doesn't give me enough to do.*
2. *My boss gives me too much to do.*
3. *My boss doesn't talk to me.*
4. *My boss doesn't like me.*
5. *I don't like my boss.*
6. *I think I've made a mistake in joining this organization.*
7. *It's a madhouse!*
8. *Something's wrong: I seem to be getting on too well!*

These are not crises in themselves but might be the symptoms of a genuine crisis in the making. And we could go on adding to this list in much the same vein. So let's look at the best- and worst-case scenarios—and leave you to fit in those which come in-between.

### THE BEST-CASE SCENARIO

It's always possible, of course, that you'll be persuaded by reasoned argument to stay longer and give yourself, the job and the organization a little longer. You'll doubtless be told you've made a good initial impression and reminded not to be impatient. *It's important to recognize that not all of us are going to make it to the top or be capable of reaching for the skies.* In your early career, the chances are you'll be reasonably ambitious and wish to compare your career progress and salary growth with the cohort of your exact contemporaries. There's nothing wrong with that, either. Except that appearances may be deceptive and the grass always looks much greener in the adjacent meadow!

## THE WORST-CASE SCENARIO

Despite careful efforts on both sides to ensure a good match between job and job-holder, a certain number of newly appointed employees in any organization will decide they've made a mistake and wish to quit before too many weeks have passed. This *initial induction crisis* generally falls in the first few weeks of starting work in a new job. Right from the outset you get the feeling you've made a mistake, that this is not for you. Yet you persevere because you've taken some trouble to land this job and you don't want to be seen to give up that easily. The symptoms nevertheless persist. You want out. How to go about it and retain your dignity?

Every worthwhile organization recognizes that mistakes take place in personnel selection and hiring, just as they do in production or maintenance or sales. Provided you're willing to discuss the reasons— not necessarily the most personal reasons, if you'd rather exclude them—then most organizations will help you to find your way into another job with another employer and there need be no hard feelings, either way. You must however be prepared for some kind of interrogation on why you feel you must leave, so soon after starting. You're bound to be asked whether you feel you've given yourself— and the organization—enough time before making this irrevocable decision to quit. The cost of replacing you could be considerable and there's a clear need for management to know how and why you and they are mismatched. You may express yourself clearly and forcefully at your 'exit interview' but avoid giving unnecessary offence. After all, you may need some kind of reference or letter to confirm that you've left the organization on good terms. Or you may wish to return at some later date!

There's no shame in admitting you've made a mistake or in deciding to quit your present job. In fact, it may be a perfectly logical course of action—though not necessarily the only one. Everything depends on you—your temperament, your health, your financial position, your own interests in life. Above all, how you feel about yourself and the organization at the end of each working day.

One reason why you might decide to quit your present company is that you've discovered you're in the wrong career! In which case, it may well be time to move out—rather than move up or move on. Before doing so, you should certainly take another long, hard, dispassionate look at yourself and your promotion prospects before deciding to move on—or move out of your present career.

This might be an excellent time to go back and talk to the career consultants who helped you think through your initial career choice and job search. They will certainly be interested to discuss with you in confidence how your career thinking has progressed since your last consultation. They should help you to evaluate your present career dilemma and be able to offer strong, independent, professional advice on the validity of what you now propose to do as a long-term move. But you must go to see them with an open mind, ready to admit that your diagnosis and prescription may be wrong. Even physicians rarely heal themselves!

Later, as your career develops, you may come to value non-working dimensions of your life and not wish to compete with others for the highest echelons of the organizational ladder. In which case, you might do a lot worse than stay put, refuse to quit, and sit it out.

## SUGGESTIONS FOR FURTHER READING

Peter Williamson: *Early Careers of 1970 Graduates*, London: Department of Employment Research Paper No. 26 (1981).

# So, how did your first years go?

*To be what we are, and to become what we are capable of becoming, is the only end of life.*

Robert Louis Stevenson (1850–1894)

Chapter 20—our final chapter—tries to do three things:

1. To gather together some of the main threads of this book.
2. To invite you to consider how far your career has already come.
3. To reflect on how much further it has to go.

This slim volume has been addressed to all job hunters everywhere, but has been written specifically with you—and all other graduates and professionals—in mind. Its intention was to make you think harder and more clearly about yourself before choosing the most appropriate career and launching yourself into that desperate search for your first paid employment.

If you've followed us thus far, you'll know that the advice and guidance we offer here is essentially practical—without too much academic theorizing and limited space devoted to sophisticated conceptual analysis. If you want to probe deeper into such matters, we offer suggestions for further reading at the end of each chapter.

So, we now come to the acid test of the book's usefulness: How much has it helped you in your choice of a suitable career? And have you succeeded in finding the right job in your chosen career field? If you have, we rejoice with you in your success! If you've not yet succeeded in finding the job you really want, we urge you not to despair. Try to keep cheerful and remain philosophical. Remember, nothing comes to those who sit at home and wait. But everything comes to those who keep on trying; the impossible simply takes a little longer!

Let's maintain the optimistic tone of the book in this final chapter and assume that you've found the ideal job which we're all eventually seeking. Before moving on, let's take stock of how far you've already come.

## THINK HOW FAR YOU'VE ALREADY COME!

We can well imagine that, when you first sat down with Chapter 1 of this book, your mind was in something of a turmoil about your career choice and how to set about a successful job search. You were certainly not alone in that! Despite the best efforts of the college Careers Advisory Service, most college graduates need more practical help and advice than the Service can ever provide. As Jean-Jacques Rousseau doubtless intended to say: All men (and some women) are born equal in their need of help — especially in the area of career choice and job search—but some need more help than others.

That need for help does not end with the receipt of your first month's pay cheque. A successful career—like a beautiful garden— needs constant attention and much nurturing to bring it to perfection. There's an inherent tendency towards chaos unless the straggly growths are kept under control.

One of the most persistent anxieties expressed by those who have just launched themselves into their first career employment is this: *Have I done the right thing—or made a ghastly mistake?* You're unlikely to know the answer to that question for some time—and, in any case, you should not rush to judgement. There's a great temptation to panic in these matters and to leap from the proverbial frying pan into the frizzling fire. Try to keep calm and take stock with these three critical questions:

- 1. *Did you set out logically and systematically to follow the career guidance we've offered you?* If you've worked your way steadily through the chapters of this book, you should have undertaken a demanding but genuinely worthwhile review of your career needs and wants.

- 2. *Have you based your choice of career on the evidence to emerge from this intense self-evaluation—or simply taken a leap in the dark?* No matter what your choice of career, there are always some aspects which make you wonder whether you've been altogether wise or sane in your choice of career. Getting your *career choice* right is much more important than getting into the *right job*. A leap in the dark may prove disastrous to your career!

- 3. *Have your found yourself the very best job you can within your chosen career field?* Perhaps you felt you must accept the first or second job offer which you received. That's understandable. It's not a good idea to spend too much time looking a gift horse in the mouth. But having tucked yourself into your first job, you can now really allow yourself time to think and feel your way forward and decide whether this really is the right job in the right organization for you. Don't be afraid to admit error. But equally, don't resign from your present job until you're fairly certain you've found that better job you were after at the outset.

## LEARNING THROUGH ERROR

Few human learning curves are steeper than those which face you at college or university when you first get down to considering your career choice and your initial job search. In a relatively short space of time—often no more than a few months—you travel from virtual ignorance or, at best, great uncertainty about your future working life—right through to seeking and finding an acceptable first job in the career of your choice.

Considering how subtle and sensitive the subject area and how many sophisticated judgements you have to make, and how many pitfalls exist for the unwary, it's hardly surprising that you make some mistakes. There's no point in grieving at length over this. We're all human—and even Homer nods. If you've already been forced to recognize that the career you've chosen is not the right one for you—that in itself constitutes invaluable learning. *Please remember that most human learning is by trial and error and that we learn more by making mistakes than by being right first time.* Making mistakes is only human; but the most successful humans are those who ensure they extract the maximum learning from every experience. It is this developed capacity for sustained learning and dynamic adaptation which is the mainspring behind the most successful careers. In the words of David Silverman:

> One may miss the way in which people's views of themselves and of their situations is the outcome of an on-going process i.e. never fully determined by one or another set of structural constraints but always in the act of 'becoming', as successive experiences shape and re-shape a subjective definition of self and society.[1]

## HOW MUCH FURTHER TO GO?

Fortunately, we cannot read the future. Who amongst us would wish to know in advance precisely what fate has in store? Most of us would rather travel hopefully and are happy to arrive in due course. On the other hand, there's a very real sense in which we can and must take charge and steer some of the most important aspects of our lives—for example, our health and personal well-being—by virtue of our diet, our lifestyle—and also, to some considerable degree, our life's work and our career satisfaction.

You can make up your mind today that you will not allow your health to be undermined by eating the wrong kinds of food, and your life ruined by the abuse of drink and drugs. In a similar way, *you can decide to take charge of your career and make it responsive to your needs.* Career decisions are seldom easy and some are especially difficult when we have to balance complex economic, social and

[1] D. Silverman: *The Theory of Organisations*, London: Heinemann (1970).

234

personal advantages and disadvantages. If things go right, we know we've made the right decision; and if they go wrong, we can seek to console ourselves with the thought that we made the best decision we could in the circumstances. To paraphrase the title of a recent British film: *Whose career is it any way?*

The answer, of course, is that *it's **your** career*—from start to finish. So, why not start the way you intend to continue and make the very best of your future career? All that remains now is to offer you our very sincere good wishes for your future career into the 21st century!

**Be strong and of good courage!**

# Index